THE LAKOTA
SWEAT LODGE
CARDS

THE LAKOTA SWEAT LODGE

CARDS

Spiritual Teachings of the Sioux

CHIEF ARCHIE FIRE LAME DEER
AND HELENE SARKIS

with Ann Louise Goulène and Wendy Meg Siegel
Illustrated by Alexander Sarkis

DESTINY BOOKS
ROCHESTER, VERMONT

Destiny Books
One Park Street
Rochester, Vermont 05767

LIBRARY OF CONGRESS CATALOGING-IN-PUBLICATION DATA
Lame Deer, Archie Fire, 1935–
    The Lakota sweat lodge cards : spiritual teachings of the Sioux / Archie Fire Lame Deer, Helene Sarkis.
      p.   cm.
    Includes index.
    ISBN 0-89281-456-X
    1. Divination. 2. Spiritual life—Miscellanea. 3. Lakota Indians—Religion and mythology—Miscellanea. 4. Lakota Indians—Sweatbaths—Miscellanea. I. Sarkis, Helene. II. Title.
BF1751.L36 1994
133.3'242–dc20
                                    93–30808
                                          CIP

Printed and bound in the United States

10 9 8 7 6 5

Text design and layout by Virginia L. Scott and Bonnie Atwater

Destiny Books is a division of Inner Traditions International

Distributed to the book trade in Canada by Publishers Group West (PGW), Toronto, Ontario

Distributed to the book trade in the United Kingdom by Deep Books, London

Distributed to the book trade in Australia by Millennium Books, Newtown, N.S.W.

Distributed to the book trade in New Zealand by Tandem Press, Auckland

DEDICATED TO

THE LAKOTA NATION
AND
ALEXANDER CRAVEN SARKIS

ACKNOWLEDGMENTS

The Lakota Sweat Lodge card deck and book grew out of personal Sweat Lodge experiences and the teachings of Chief Archie Fire Lame Deer, who acted as consultant and advisor on the project. The deck was created through the collaboration of three women who shared Inipi experiences and Lakota Sioux spiritual teachings with Chief Lame Deer and who also support one another in a Full Moon Circle and other spiritual rituals. The spirit voices, traditions, and card spread guidance and meditation texts were by Ann Louise Goulène; the card interpretive texts and spread concepts were the work of Wendy Meg Siegel. Our intent is to share, through the ancient and graphic medium of divinatory cards, some of the power, insight, release, and guidance we have found through the Sweat Lodge and other native teachings.

We give special acknowledgment to our Full Moon sisters, who created a circle of love and energy to empower us: Zoe Blatchley, Meegan Burt, Rosemary Ceraso, Janet Hand, Joan Keenan, Val Le Gaspi, Heidi McClure, Llynn Newman, and Puja Tobey.

Our special thanks also to Patrice Benneward for typing the manuscript and to Amanda Goulène for her loving support and patience.

CONTENTS

PART II • THE EIGHT SUPERNATURALS

PART III • THE ELEMENTS OF THE SWEAT LODGE

PREFACE

Some of us have had the privilege of experiencing the Sweat Lodge, the Inipi Purification Ceremony. For those who have not had this opportunity or wish for more knowledge and understanding, we set forth in these words and images a symbol of our respect and love for the Lodge and the traditional teachings, as shared with us by Chief Archie Fire Lame Deer.

The current availability of native American teachings, sweats, and seminars is unprecedented. Until the American Indian Religious Freedom Act, passed in the late 1970s during the Carter Administration, traditional religious ceremony was forbidden both on and off reservations. The ongoing struggle for comprehensive protection of all native religions is today led by Senator Inouye of Hawaii.

The changes set in motion by Chief Archie Fire Lame Deer, who was instrumental in effecting the act, have aroused worldwide interest in and awareness of native American religions. Many tribes and "medicine" people are sharing their ancient ceremonies with the larger world in order to encourage and assist us to reconnect with the consciousness of our natural relationship with the Earth Mother and all her inhabitants.

At the core of all native American teachings is one message: to walk in balance with the Earth. All ritual and ceremony is geared toward creating awareness of this intimate balance with the seen and unseen forces of the Earth Mother.

What we see today in the onslaught of native American awareness workshops, seminars, Vision Quests, and sweats is sometimes an eclectic distortion of tradition. While these events may provide valuable experiences, much wisdom of the ancient knowledge and richness of tradition flounders or is completely lost. As with the Inipi, or Sweat Lodge, the beauty, power, and sacredness of the ceremony is often distilled and distorted.

In his tribe, Minneconju Sioux—Rosebud Reservation —Chief Archie Fire Lame Deer, from the lineage of the Lame Deer and Quick Bear families, has the distinction of being Wichasha Wakan, or Holy Man; he is a Man of Dreams. Chief Lame Deer, whose views are the basis of the teachings presented in this book, brings with him a rich legacy of traditional Sweat-Lodge teachings. These traditions represent the unique heritage of the Lame Deer and Quick Bear families and thus may differ from teachings based on anthropological research or from other native teachers.

The sacred Inipi ceremony is an ancient ritual of healing and purification that has existed in the Lakota (Sioux) culture for thousands of years.

This book, with its set of teaching cards, combines the lessons and symbols of the Inipi ceremony with Spirit voices, traditional interpretations of meaning, and meditations to provide you with a personal tool for inner growth and transformation. As with any spiritual work, you are the source, you are the vehicle. Nothing is more powerful than your own inner knowing.

My first Lodge experience was quite startling and fateful. Although I had always been interested in native American lore, particularly of the Sioux, and dreamed of someday visiting the Black Hills, fate quite literally brought the Inipi Lodge to me.

An Inipi seminar was sponsored by someone in our women's group, and a lodge was built in our local nature preserve. We were all interested and excited to meet a real Indian and experience a Sweat Lodge. My brother had known Archie Fire and told me many interesting and funny stories about him, so I was eager to meet him.

I fell ill a week before the seminar and was hospitalized. I thought I would be unable to attend the seminar, but I was. Spirit prepared me in the traditional way— fasting and praying for four days before the lodge.

I entered that lodge with all my insecurities and fears and left having experienced a vision that allayed all fear and illuminated my path. This was not a Vision Quest on a mountain but surely a gift from Spirit, whose power and reality is hard to convey.

My love of the teachings, the Lodge, the ceremonies, and the Lakota people grew over the years as our group continued to sponsor seminars and Inipi ceremonies with Chief Lame Deer. Out of my profession as a graphic designer grew the concept of these teaching cards. The cards convey the beauty and power of the Spirit forces and the traditions related to the Inipi Lodge.

The Lodge has given me a true path of connection to the Earth—feeling safe on the earth and in the woods, forests, and wetlands. It taught me to be quiet, to listen to the soft Spirit voices in nature, and to see the reflection of God in every leaf and stone. It helped me find my place in relation to our brothers and sisters on the earth— insects, animals, birds, plants, humans, all put here by the Creator to coexist in a symphony of life. It has helped me to see time with a new understanding, for there are no clocks in the Spirit World.

The Lodge is community, connection to spirit, inward vision. The Lodge is to pray in the darkness full of flickering lights, to feel the prayer ties hanging over one's head, hundreds of packets of prayers offered to the air and fire to rise up to the Great Spirit. The Lodge is the pungent aroma of sage, sweet grass, tobacco; it is singing the sacred songs that connect one to ancestors and spirits thousands of years old. The Lodge is prayer, thanksgiving, laughter, tears—the visible movement of healing and the purification of spirit.

Helene Sarkis

INTRODUCTION

*Memories of the time past . . . time to be . . . ancients . . .
grandfathers and grandmothers . . . my people know time not
by the sound of bells and chimes but by passing from one
strong experience to another. Vitalizers appearing; snow; rain;
hail; sleet and tears; preparing the Inipi; Grandfather's breath.
Into Purification Ceremony, also known by people as Sweat
Lodge. The care we take in preparation is for that which gives
us new life. . . . When the sun reaches its zenith, we begin by
assembling the sacred fire. . . . As the sun begins to set, we
have all arrived to share and bond and go into Mother Earth's
womb to begin again . . . breathing Wakan Tanka's breath.
Together we start by purifying and sharing the Sacred Pipe.
We talk about the Holy Woman who brought us the seven rituals of this Sacred Pipe, the bondage of all humanity and peace
upon the Mother Earth; Pté San Wi, the ancient name of the
Holy Woman, who transformed herself from a cloud and
became a white bison . . . long ago, yet still alive today. . . . We
gather together to let that which burdens us be released. . . .*

We talk of ancient stones still standing covered by moss. Long forgotten by modern man, we talk about how we can bring that back together again. The days are no longer counted. We talk about ancient ceremonies, the ghost dance and how the earth will roll up to reveal the flowering tree again. . . . We see in our dreams and visions little spirit lights from nowhere as they whisper their secrets to our souls. . . . We tell of those who go up on the mountains, naked with only a quilt of stars to clothe and shelter them. The Mother Earth becomes our bed, the cloud our cover; seekers of truth with no one between us but that which created us. Looking at the sun, we dance, piercing our flesh, praying for our sisters, who give life in pain. Tears streaming down our cheeks so generations to come might live, we come to know the grandfather who hears all . . . and our mother who hears all . . . the children among us free to laugh and run without the sound of anger and limit. . . . When the song is done, we rise with the sun to enter the womb once again. We emerge knowing that we are returning to our lives with a vision . . . of ourselves.

The English term *Sweat Lodge* hardly conveys the meaning of the sacred Inipi Purification Ceremony. In the Lakota language, *Inipo* means "you should purify yourself." We purify ourselves in the Inipi Lodge before any sacred rite.

To enter a Sweat Lodge is to be born again; while there, one prays to combine the physical, the spiritual, and the mental. Praying is not a recitation of words: We do not want your prayers to come from memory or from a book. We want your prayers to come from the depth of your heart, not from your head.

This book shares some of the meanings, teachings, and traditions of the Sweat Lodge that have been with our people for thousands of years. We do this work to reawaken awareness in our own peoples who have lost contact with their native traditions and because the Lodge ceremony is now being shared with the world (as was predicted by our prophets long ago).

Let us learn to open our spirits, to be patient, and to help one another. These are the teachings of the Sweat Lodge ceremony: to follow the path of reunification; to gather people together and reflect upon what we can do for the Earth Mother, not what more we can take from her.

Our God is your God, only our God is called and approached in a different way.

> Mitakuye Oyasin
> for all my relations
> Chief Archie Fire Lame Deer

SONG OF THE BLACK TAIL DEER

In the very beginning of life
my life was that of the herb.
I lived of the herb and the plants and
the trees and the roots,
but that life has gone.

Then my life was that of the buffalo.
I lived of the buffalo-sustained life for clothing,
for warmth in the winter, the spring.
In ceremonies, in prayers,
my life is that of the buffalo,
but that life has gone.

My life is that of the white man.
I do things like the white man,
I talk like the white man,
I dress like the white man,
and that life has gone.
That life was in the world of materialism.
A new generation has come.

My life is that of the black tail deer.
I will go back to the top of the mountains;
there I will replenish myself.
I will come back with the morning star
to purify the waters,
and after I purify the waters,
I will return back to the top of the mountain,
and at the end of time
I will return to replenish the earth.
I am the black tail deer.
A new nation made up of all colors of man
for you to see.
The black tail deer really is a brown deer after all.

Chief Archie Fire Lame Deer
(Sacred Song)

THE SACRED INIPI

Lakota tradition teaches that the Inipi Purification Ceremony was brought to the people by Kanka, the Old Woman Sorceress, so they could purify themselves physically, mentally, emotionally, and spiritually. The White Buffalo Calf Woman, symbol of purity and renewal, brought the gift and knowledge of the Sacred Pipe. These two concepts—object and ceremony, symbol and ritual—are at the core of all Lakota spiritual beliefs.

The seven sacred ceremonies of the Lakota are the Inipi Lodge, Vision Quest, Sun Dance, Making of Relatives, Keeping of the Ghost, Coming of Age, and Throwing of the Ball. These ceremonies weave the fabric of Lakota life. But it is the Sacred Pipe and Sweat Lodge that create balance. They represent prayer and purification and they are integral to all ceremonies and to life itself.

The Inipi lodge is a place of release, vision, and redemption. The focus of prayers there is not on the self but on all creation; to move beyond egocentrism and merge with the Earth Mother and the other elemental forces of Sun, Fire, Air, and Water; to feel oneself a tiny part of creation and yet an integral part of the universe. In the lodge, we pray for others—therefore we pray for ourselves. The Great Spirit resembles all that He has created.

Physically, the lodge is a small dome constructed from bent willow saplings in a prescribed and sacred pattern. From below, the shape of the dome depicts the morning stars: the planets and their polarities—the supernatural forces. The sixteen willow branches enter the ground at points that represent the Sixteen Great Mysteries of the Lakota Creation. From above, the pattern symbolizes the universe, all creation, and the Spirit forces within it.

In the center of the lodge is a fire pit used for heated stones that are brought inside in prescribed numbers and sequences. Earth taken from the fire pit forms the altar mound. The willow dome is covered with skins or tarps. A person enters through the small door flap on hands and knees, symbolizing a return to the womb of Mother Earth.

INIPI PURIFICATION CEREMONY

There are many types and lengths of Lodge ceremonies, but the simplest and most powerful is the Purification Lodge. It consists of four "doors," or rounds, after which the door flap is opened. At the beginning of each round, heated rocks are brought in, and herbs— sweet grass, sage, and cedar—are sprinkled on them along with water, which creates a great steam referred to as Grandfather's Breath. The Wichasha Wakan's (Holy

Man's) prayers, the sacred songs, and the intense, purify-ing steam transport one from a small, dark hut to the vast cathedral of the inner world. This intimate space, crowded with other seekers, becomes the Earth Mother's bosom, where she nurtures all her children, and a high altar, where we offer our prayers and small sufferings to the Creator in grateful thanksgiving.

The discomforts of extreme heat and sweating some-how detach the mind from its narrow identification with the body and create a connection with an expanded vision of one's self, one's purpose, and one's relation to the conscious world and to the Spirit World. The leader, or Holy Man, is the vital balancer of energies, positive and negative, the energy of the people in the lodge and of the spirits who also enter.

Prayers, sacred songs, and teachings are shared during the ceremony. Personal inner issues can emerge through one's physical position in the lodge—the position of each lodge pole in relationship to its construction is related to a Spirit Power and its realm of influence (see the Wheel of the Lodge illustration). The Wheel of the Lodge, which symbolizes creation, evolution, and the aspiration toward spiritual consciousness in the material world, locates the position of the Spirit Gods.

THE SPIRIT GODS AND THE SUPERNATURALS

The Sixteen Great Mysteries (the aspects of Wakan Tanka), weave themselves through the rich tapestry of Lakota tradition by means of stories, the Ohunt akan.

The tradition is an oral one, and countless intricate tales about the interactions and deeds of the Spirit Gods have been handed down, elaborated on, and used to illustrate moral lessons by implication. It is not the purpose of this book to fully describe the many aspects and teachings of the Spirit Gods and Supernaturals but to instead evoke their essential characteristics to create for the reader a powerful image and connection with the card meanings.

Nothing has but one meaning or aspect; everything has polarity—the dark and light, the negative and positive. Duality is the present state of consciousness that the mind and soul must escape in order to walk in balance, to transcend the illusions of this world and realize oneness with the Great Spirit. Inherent in all ceremonies is the potential for the experience of duality, as is found in all life. Duality describes opposites—as in the Oriental concept of yin and yang, as in male and female, light and dark—which together create the whole.

Positive and negative spirits are invited into the Lodge to act in concert to point out our weaknesses, flaws, strengths, and gifts. It is the purpose of the Supernaturals to force us to see our various aspects, to own and honor our duplicities as part of being human, and to guide us to understanding, change, true wholeness, and balance.

WHEEL OF THE LODGE

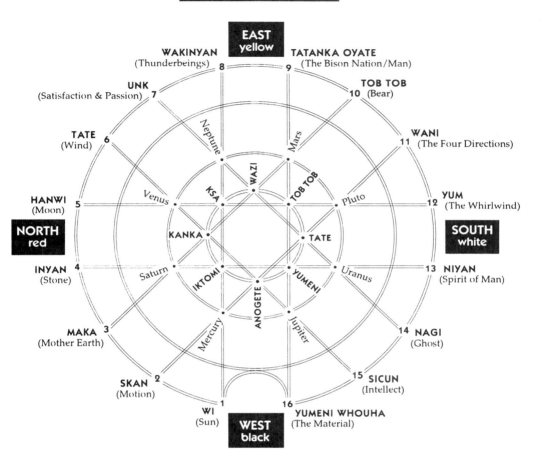

SIXTEEN GREAT MYSTERIES IN THE SWEAT LODGE

1-4 Superiors   5-8 Associates   9-12 Subordinates   13-16 Inferiors

EIGHT SUPERNATURALS

Positive Forces	Negative Forces
Mercury	ANOGETE, *Woman with Two Faces*
Saturn	IKTOMI, *Spider*
Venus	KANKA, *Old Woman Sorceress*
Neptune	KSA, *Goddess of Water*
Mars	WAZI, *Old Man Sorcerer of the North*
Pluto	TOB TOB, *Eight Directions of the Wind*
Uranus	TATE, *Wind*
Jupiter	YUMENI, *Whirlwind & Storm*

THE CREATION

Superior Spirits

Wakan Tanka, the Great Spirit, reflected upon himself and created the four Superior Spirits: Wi, Skan, Maka, and Inyan.

SUPERIORS

1. WI, *Sun*	The first to be created, bringing light to the world.
2. SKAN, *Motion*	The motion of the universe, the lifeblood pulse of the body, the solar winds.
3. MAKA, *Mother Earth*	The Spirit Maka took the form of the earth; Skan drew upon the earth to create the streams and oceans.
4. INYAN, *Stone*	The Spirit Inyan became the solid support of the earth or the rock associated with the natural forces of the earth.

These four emanations of God—Wakan Tanka, All That Is—over time no longer functioned as pure spirit. In due course, they took material form and also manifested or created companions from their own essence.

Associate Spirits

The Superior Spirits created the Associate Spirits: Hanwi, Tate, Unk, and Wakinyan.

ASSOCIATES

5. HANWI, *Moon*	Created as companion to the Sun and

	to light the dark side of the Earth; Skan, the essence of vitality and movement, set the Moon in motion opposite the Sun.
6. TATE, *Wind*	Skan created Tate to assist him in forming the winds that blow across the earth, creating storms, tornadoes, and tempests.
7. UNK, *Satisfaction & Passion*	Maka, the flowering Mother Earth, created from her essence the beautiful Spirit Unk—passion, the pleasures and satisfactions of life, the female energy of the earth.
8. WAKINYAN, *Thunderbeings*	The essence of equilibrium, created the Winged Ones, the Thunderbeings, the purifiers or elemental electrical forces.

Subordinate Spirits

The next spirits to be created were the Subordinates: Tatanka Oyate, Tob Tob, Wani, and Yum.

SUBORDINATES	
9. TATANKA OYATE, *The Bison Nation/Man*	Tatanka, Man; Oyate Pté, The Buffalo People: Humanity's covenant was to serve God and to communicate and live in balance with the animal world and Mother Earth. The underworld was the original home of the Buffalo Nation.
10. TOB TOB, *Bear*	The Bear Spirit symbolizes wisdom— the wisdom and kinship of the Great

Spirit to the animal kingdom, the four leggeds, creeping crawlers, and winged ones.

11. WANI, *The Four Directions*

Tate created five sons from himself. Their names were Yata, Yapa, Yap, Okaga, and Eya. They lived and traveled across the earth, the first four creating the grasses and plants and the Cardinal Points—West, North, East, and South. Eya became Mahpia, the clouds that conceal the Wakinyan. They established the dimensions of time and space.

12. YUM, *The Whirlwind*

Yum, or Yumeni Wi, is the patron of love, amusement, chance, and games. She is known as The Whirlwind. She symbolizes all the circular movement of the Earth, the Moon, the Stars. She brings tornadoes and earthquakes.

Inferior Spirits

The next spirits created were the Inferiors: Niyan, Nagi, Sicun, and Yumeni Whouha.

INFERIORS

13. NIYAN, *Spirit of Man*

The spiritual essence that advises the conduct of individual humans—the eternal soul that never stops traveling the circle of life.

14. NAGI, *Ghost*

The shade or ghost between the physical world and the world of transcendent spirits; the intermediate world of those who have not finished their cycle of life in a good way.

| 15. SICUN, *Intellect* | The potency separating human beings from the animal world. With this came the knowledge of right and wrong. |
| 16. YUMENI WHOUHA, *The Material* | The physical substance of the universe. The Creator gave humans all that is necessary for survival, along with the capacity to live without accumulating the unnecessary. |

SUPERNATURAL SPIRITS

The planets are considered positive, or light, forces because they are reflectors of the Sun's energies. The Supernaturals on the inner ring of the Wheel of the Lodge represent the opposite or polarized energy. In this case, the planets are light (positive) and the Supernaturals are dark (negative), not in the sense of good and evil but rather the light and dark energies that comprise the whole of creation.

SUPERNATURALS

17. ANOGETE	*Woman with Two Faces*	Mercury
18. IKTOMI	*Spider*	Saturn
19. KANKA	*Old Woman Sorceress*	Venus
20. KSA	*Goddess of Water*	Neptune
21. WAZI	*Old Man Sorcerer of the North*	Mars
22. TOB TOB	*Eight Directions of the Wind*	Pluto
23. TATE	*Wind*	Uranus
24. YUMENI	*Whirlwind & Storm*	Jupiter

The visible planets that rise over the horizon at dawn are called the morning stars. The Supernatural Spirits are associated with the planets in a pattern of positive and negative polarities. The great, slow, regal movements of the planets have become endowed with human attributes. Cosmic emanations rain down on earth and influence human consciousness, not as Fate but as seasons and cycles in time; the potential exists to use these energies for good or ill. The Supernatural Spirits confuse, challenge, and trick us into greater understanding. They teach us to laugh at ourselves.

The measure of growth in consciousness can be seen in how we meet our challenges. Humanity's gift and task is always, through free will, to intuit and learn from patterns, to create our reality in alignment with the God-self within. The Lakota belief system holds that one can achieve happiness and fulfillment only through harmony with the natural order—living in balance with that which God has set upon the earth. The forces of the natural world—the Spirit World—are all around, only waiting to guide us, whispering softly. Listen to this ancient wisdom.

WAKAN TANKA

The Great Spirit
God resembles all that He has created.

THE SIXTEEN GREAT MYSTERIES

◄ SUPERIORS ►

1	2	3	4
WI	**SKAN**	**MAKA**	**INYAN**
Sun	*Motion*	*Mother Earth*	*Stone*

◄ ASSOCIATES ►

5	6	7	8
HANWI	**TATE**	**UNK**	**WAKINYAN**
Moon	*Wind*	*Satisfaction*	*Thunderbeings*
		& Passion	

◄ SUBORDINATES ►

9	10	11	12
TATANKA	**TOB TOB**	**WANI**	**YUM**
OYATE	*Bear*	*The Four*	*The Whirlwind*
The Bison		*Directions*	
Nation/Man			

◄ INFERIORS ►

13	14	15	16
NIYAN	**NAGI**	**SICUN**	**YUMENI**
Spirit of Man	*Ghost*	*Intellect*	**WHOUHA**
			The Material

THE SUPERNATURALS

17	18	19	20
ANOGETE	**IKTOMI**	**KANKA**	**KSA**
Woman with	*Spider*	*Old Woman*	*Goddess of*
Two Faces	Saturn	*Sorceress*	*Water*
Mercury		Venus	Neptune

21	22	23	24
WAZI	**TOB TOB**	**TATE**	**YUMENI**
Old Man	*Eight*	*Wind*	*Whirlwind*
Sorcerer of	*Directions*	Uranus	*& Storm*
the North	*of the Wind*		Jupiter
Mars	Pluto		

THE CARDS

THE SIXTEEN GREAT MYSTERIES

GREAT MYSTERIES	CARD MEANING
0. WAKAN TANKA, *Great Spirit*	The Source
1. WI, *Sun*	Personal Power
2. SKAN, *Motion*	Manifestation
3. MAKA, *Mother Earth*	Birth
4. INYAN, *Stone*	Support
5. HANWI, *Moon*	Reflection
6. TATE, *Wind*	Change
7. UNK, *Satisfaction & Passion*	To Walk in Balance
8. WAKINYAN, *Thunderbeings*	Energy
9. TATANKA OYATE, *The Bison Nation/Man*	Attainment
10. TOB TOB, *Bear*	Wisdom
11. WANI, *The Four Directions*	Lessons
12. YUM, *The Whirlwind*	Love
13. NIYAN, *Spirit of Man*	Higher Self
14. NAGI, *Ghost*	Shadow Self
15. SICUN, *Intellect*	Discernment
16. YUMENI WHOUHA, *The Material*	Abundance

SUPERNATURALS

SUPERNATURAL SPIRITS	CARD MEANING	PLANET
17. ANOGETE, *Woman with Two Faces*	Duality	Mercury
18. IKTOMI, *Spider*	Fear of the Unseen	Saturn
19. KANKA, *Old Woman Sorceress*	Dreams	Venus
20. KSA, *Goddess of Water*	Uncover	Neptune
21. WAZI, *Old Man Sorcerer of the North*	Resolution	Mars
22. TOB TOB, *Eight Directions of the Wind*	Self-protection	Pluto
23. TATE, *Wind*	Self-expression	Uranus
24. YUMENI, *Whirlwind & Storm*	Focus	Jupiter

ELEMENTS OF THE SWEAT LODGE

ELEMENTS	CARD MEANING
25. MAHPIA, *Cloud*	Compulsions/Addictions
26. SAPA, *The West—Black*	Meditate
27. LUTA, *The North—Red*	Renewal
28. GI, *The East—Yellow*	Clarity
29. OKAGA SKA, *The South—White*	Growth
30. INIPI, *Sweat Lodge*	Purification
31. CHUNUPA WAKAN, *The Sacred Pipe*	Prayer
32. CHA WAKAN, *Tree of Life*	Acceptance
33. AHPO WI CHAPI, *Morning Star*	Hope
34. TUNKASILA ONIWAN, *Grandfather's Breath*	Faith
35. PEJUTA WAKAN, *Sacred Herbs*	Healing

36. CHANLI WAPAKTA,   Social Consciousness
    Prayer Ties
37. OLOWANPI, *Sacred Songs*   Harmony
38. PITA HOCHOKAN, *The Fire Pit*   Motivation
39. MITAKUYE OYASIN,   Respect
    All My Relations
40. HOCHOKAN WAKAN,   Reverence
    Sacred Mound
41. MINI, *Water*   Creativity
42. NIYAN, *Air*   Life Force
43. PITA, *Fire*   Eternal Life
44. MAKA, *Earth*   Nurturing
45. WAGLE SHUN, *The Swan*   Peace
46. UNCI, *Grandmother*   Female Power
47. EYESHINU TI, *Moontime*   Spiritual Power
48. WAHINHAYA, *The Mole*   Regeneration
49. HANBLECHEYA,   Vision
    Crying for a Dream

NOTES ON DIVINATION AND SYNCHRONICITY

Divination is any technique used to connect with a "higher," supraconscious self or God-self for insights and answers. This experience can range from an inner knowing, a prayer, a meditation, or a deliberate technique to induce a state of altered consciousness where symbols and information are readily accessible. Everyone has this connection to higher consciousness, but there are various names, belief systems, and degrees to which people relate to this vehicle.

Cultures throughout history have used divination, oracle, or predictive systems: the Hebrew Oracle of the Temple; Egyptian Mystery Schools; the Oracle of Delphi;

Roman, Christian, and Medieval priests; visionaries; seers; shamans; holy men; medicine men. The techniques have ranged from reading entrails, cast bones, yarrow stick patterns, and tarot cards to using astrology, card systems, and psychic information.

People seek answers beyond their normal range of consciousness. They use divination techniques to access that information. The ways in which divination works have been variously described in terms of our connection to Spirit—through angels, guides, higher beings, as a product of the mathematic structure of the universe, or as our connection with the collective unconscious.

Dr. Carl Jung proposed that divination rests on the concept of synchronicity. Synchronicity is the simultaneous occurrence of a complex of significant events or symbols. These symbols or events occur at a certain precise moment in time, as with card layouts. Jung proposed that physical and psychic realms coincide within a synchronistic event and that these realms must also be (somewhere) a unified reality, that is, one reality of the physical and psychic realms, Unis Mundis, the One World.

The basis of divination rests in synchronicity but is also related to the modern-day physics concept of the unified field theory. There is in a moment of time a cluster of events—physical and psychic. The scientific discovery that the intent or "mind" of the researcher influences the outcome of an experiment raises the corresponding concept of how we influence our reality: by accessing information from a "higher source," creating new intent and physical reality from our information and perceptions.

The coincidence or synchronicity of selecting cards that have the appropriate message or meaning is sometimes uncanny. The process is actually directed by the supra-conscious mind that is connected to all knowledge of one's self and the world or reality one sees. If this supra-conscious mind or spirit were activated at all times, one would be flooded with myriad perceptions, and the process of living, absorbing, processing, and reflecting on information would be impossible. The state of consciousness that is evoked through divination, meditation, and prayer is reserved for deepening perceptions, for guidance, and for self-exploration.

Regardless of one's personal belief system, these teachings, meditation cards, and native American concepts are useful for illuminating issues, patterns, problems, and answers. Native Americans would perhaps describe divination in and through the signs and symbols of the natural world as messages from Spirit experienced through the belief that everything is alive, that everything has consciousness and is part of the Great Spirit. If one believes that everything is consciousness, then the path of prayer, introspection, and meditation can lead you to your own inner answers.

HOW TO USE THE CARDS

Divination systems are often used when one is troubled or in a crisis. Lakota Sweat Lodge cards, if used regularly and consistently, afford a blossoming reconnection with Earth Spirit. Layouts and meditations done when one is balanced and untroubled afford new levels of insight. Recording symbols is very useful—in our busy lives we sometimes forget or ignore the symbols and gifts we receive each day. Interpretation of the cards is, of course, highly subjective. After trying a few of the simpler layouts, daily cards, or weekly meditations, you will trust more of your intuitive or instinctive knowing.

Throughout our lives we grow in the illusion of our separateness of all that surrounds us. Divination allows us to perceive the larger pattern of which we are a part. When confronted with a decision, or a sense of being lost or confused, when seeking confirmation of that which we sense to be right action, we can use these cards to provide the missing clues, the fuller perspective, and the voices of support we need.

Keeping a journal of your queries and replies, though not essential, will yeild benefits. The act of writing out your question allows the mind to become settled and focused. Also, you become aware of your true feelings. For example, you may inquire about moving to a particular locale, but in wording the question and applying a time factor to it, you may discover that you really do not imagine yourself connected to that place far into the future. In this way you are led to focus your questions and concerns more clearly and gain the clearest insights from the cards chosen.

In addition to the Spirit voices, traditions, and card interpretations, each card has a meditation that may be used as an affirmation and as a pathway into one's personal relationship with the heart of the Spirit presented.

The card spreads presented in this book are particularly designed for the self-exploration required to know oneself as a part of the larger pattern. In choosing a spread, read the paragraph preceding each. There you will find a theme containing key words that will stimulate a response in you. Is this a matter of transformation and rebirth (Firekeeper's Walk spread), or a matter of rebalancing (Elemental spread), or an issue requiring knowledge of relationship (Tree of Life spread)? Use your inner response to choose an appropriate spread.

Pose your question as "what do I need to know?" about the issue rather than asking for a yes or no—the answer will be a broader response.

After choosing a layout that suits your current situation, sit quietly and center yourself, holding the cards between your hands with the left palm facing up and the right palm facing down. Allow your energy to merge with the cards. Do the focusing meditation below and then shuffle the cards.

Draw from the top of the shuffled deck or lay the cards in a fan shape, face down, and choose the cards you are drawn to.

FOCUSING MEDITATION

You are about to enter a Lodge. You may have an issue to resolve or you may wish to give thanks to the Creator and receive whatever illumination Spirit gifts to you. This Lodge has been prepared in a sacred way, and the collective effort of many has prepared this place for you. The intent of all is to pray and share in a good way. Imagine you are returning to the womb of Mother Earth as you kneel to enter the lodge and find your place within the circle. The stone people are ready, and the one who pours the water, the Wichasha Wickan, creates the great steam that is your grandfather's breath. You reflect and now pose your question or prayer to the Great Spirit, All That Is.

DAILY CARD MEDITATION

Center yourself using the focusing meditation above, and use an issue you need guidance with or ask for a symbol on your path. Shuffle the deck, spread the cards in a fan, and select one. Use the card to indicate the issue for reflection as a visual meditation. Explore the issue it raises. Record meditation or daily cards for an overview of patterns and guidance.

WEEKLY CARD MEDITATION

After centering and meditation, select three cards to create a theme for the week—an issue to address or process over a period of time. Each card represents one of the following concepts:

1. Outer Work: One's relation to the world, friends, family, relationships, career, and what these relationships mirror back to us. This card represents what we need to give others.

2. Inner Work: One's personal goals, dreams, processes of creativity, pleasures, self-nurturing; what we need to remember, what we need to give ourselves.

3. Spirit Work: One's relation to the developing consciousness of one's higher or spirit self and connec-

tion and service to the Great Spirit; what we need to give to God.

Read the Spirit voices and card meanings in the book, and reflect on the message at the beginning of the week. Observe and record any synchronicities during the week (that is, a repeat of the symbols involved), and start the week with a clear intent to work with these symbols or messages in your life.

EXAMPLE

Issue: *On my career path, what do I need to know or do right now?*

OUTER WORK	INNER WORK	SPIRIT WORK
EYESHINU TI,	HANBLECHEYA,	CHA WAKAN,
Moontime	*Crying for a Dream*	*Tree of Life*
Spiritual Power	Vision	Acceptance

Outer Work: To meditate on and acknowledge the power inherent in woman to create and manifest what she needs; to trust this power more and to bring this knowledge and power into outer world dealings—business and interpersonal relationships.

Inner Work: To acknowledge and nurture the inner wellsprings to truth and creativity, to take more time to nurture that inner vision. Retreat and renew one's relationship to the inner self.

Spirit Work: To meditate on patience and acceptance —the fruits of labors ripening in their own time. Acknowledge that though each leaf of the Tree of Life is individual, it is a part of the overall beauty of the whole.

NEW-MOON MEDITATION

As native American consciousness is so closely attuned to the earth and the procession of the seasons, we can also align to the rhythm of each passing month with a meditation layout on the day of the new or full moon (see below).

Draw two cards. The first card reflects the issue ended, completed, or resolved in the last light of the waning moon. The second card reflects the issue or theme to bring to the light, using the dark energy of the new moon—a time of new beginnings. Reflect on the inner connection the cards' images and writings bring up. There is no question asked here—it is rather a gift of insight on unseen processes.

FULL-MOON MEDITATION

Draw four cards, each representing a phase of the moon for the month: new, waxing, full, waning. The gift of reflection asked for here is to see a pattern, rhythm, plan, or focus of direction for the coming month.

EXAMPLE

NEW	WAXING	FULL	WANING
LUTA,	WAGLE SHUN,	YUM, *The*	HANWI,
The North	*The Swan*	*Whirlwind*	*Moon*
Renewal	Peace	Love	Reflection

This selection reflects a particularly strong message about balance. The cards suggest a pattern of Renewal, Peace, Love, and Reflections, concepts that easily get lost under pressure. The building energy from the new to the full moon should therefore focus on renewal: refocusing of energies, creating time for oneself and those practices that keep you in balance. Concentrate on the concept of peace, regardless of what is happening around you, at full moon when energy peaks, balancing events with love. The waning period till next moon suggests reflection, introspection, and consciousness of the month's lessons and any new pattern revealed.

CARD SPREADS

The following card spreads can be used with the Lakota Sweat Lodge cards. Choose a layout that suits your current situation and the type of guidance you seek. Or choose just one card—as a lesson for the day or to receive direction in a specific area of your life.

Before laying out the cards, sit quietly and center yourself (use the focusing meditation on page 22), holding the deck between both hands with the left palm facing up and the right palm down. Allow your mind to merge with the essence of the cards. Then shuffle the deck. When choosing cards, mentally ask to be guided to the cards with the most beneficial lesson for you.

FOUR DIRECTIONS SPREAD

The Four Directions spread is especially suitable for cyclical issues—for example, relationships, health, the coming year, the week, the day—and, in order to gain a "well-rounded" perspective, to find the circle hidden within a situation.

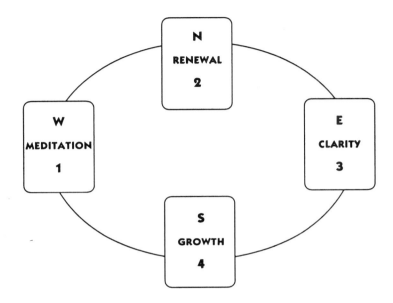

Remember that all life is a circle. Use the spread as a map that can give you your bearings in unclear terrain. Allow yourself time to hear the message coming to you from each direction. Then allow the messages to blend into a circle of meaning that will guide your next steps.

1. The West—Meditation: The West is the place of beginnings. It is Bear's dark den, where she retreats, newly pregnant, into a long, silent, and dreamlike conversation with Mother Earth. Her belly grows larger with new life. She awakens with this life issuing from her and a great hunger that drives her out into the world for satisfaction.

    The card in the position of the West indicates an important aspect of the issue presented that needs to be brought into quiet contemplation, away from the distractions of the world. Place this aspect within the unlimited sanctuary of your meditation. Allow insights and ideas, connections and progressions, to rise into your heart and mind. Allow the new life that is asking you for your nurturing to grow within you until it can express its nature and truth, first within the silence of yourself and then in the light of the world.

2. The North—Renewal: The North is the place of the Vitalizers, the purifying snows and the bracing winds. It is the place of wisdom that comes when "snow" appears on one's head as white hair. It is vigor, skill, and wise humor.

   The card in the position of the North offers you a path for revitalization of the issue presented. It reminds you to use your learned and innate wisdom with a lightness of heart and a good deal of humor. When we can genuinely laugh at ourselves, we are restoring the vitality lost through stress and worry. This is how we accept the gifts of the North, renewing ourselves in spirit. Like Wazi, we become old but not aged.

3. The East—Clarity: The East is the place of clear light as the arms of Wi embrace Maka anew each dawn. Wi brings light to what has been in darkness and gives to the Earth the energy to produce life.

   The card in the position of the East brings to light a message of clarity, allowing new vision and understanding to dawn in your consciousness. Thus may a new beginning, a fresh starting place, become apparent to you regarding the issue presented.

Allow the message of this card to rise in your consciousness like the sun lifting over the horizon, lighting more and more terrain, giving definition to what was once in shadow and providing the energy that excites new life into action.

4. The South—Growth: The South is the place of Okaga Ska, doorkeeper of between-the-worlds. It is the place of innocent wonder and knowing and of all things green and growing. It is spontaneity and joy and acceptance of all that is as the body of Wakan Tanka.

    The card in the position of the South tells you where you will find fertile ground that will nourish your new perspective. It tells of that which will support your new growth with the honor and joy it deserves.

ELEMENTAL SPREAD

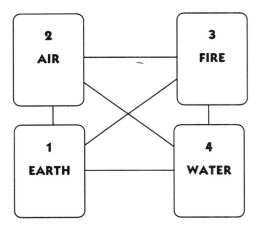

Earth, air, fire, and water are the sustainers of life. Through these we are given all that we need to live.

Sometimes, in the hurry and pressure of our days, we forget to take care of our needs and an imbalance occurs. This imbalance impacts us in subtle yet pervasive ways.

Using the Elemental spread allows you to look at your relationship with the four cornerstones of life. By repeating this spread periodically, one may come to recognize the shifts of attention through which rebalancing occurs.

1. Earth: The earth brings forth great abundance for nourishment. Wherever on the surface of this great globe one lives, all nutrients are available through various forms. Are you nourishing yourself in all ways, or is a vital "nutrient" missing from your diet of life? The card drawn for this position addresses an area in, or manner by, which you may increase the health and vitality of your body, mind, and spirit.

2. Air: Air is the most immediate sustainer of life. We take in the fresh gift of the green exhalation and life force with each breath. Are you able to inhale this gift deep into your body and being, or are you restricted by tension or fear? By pursuing the message of this card, you will find a path into the full expansion of your lungs, mind, and spirit, which so energized may then express the full beauty of your being.

3. Fire: Fire consumes and restores, leaving fresh new ground and energy for growth. Our internal fires provoke action beyond that which is familiar, motivating us into new areas of growth. Are you giving

fuel to your fires or simply stocking the coals for some future, more convenient time? Is your fire burning out of control, indiscriminately consuming all in its path? This card addresses the ways in which you are presently using your "fire" energy, offering either encouragement or redirection.

4. Water: Water is vital to the homeostasis of the body, regulating blood pressure and waste elimination and maintaining cellular integrity. It is also the flow of emotion, of creativity, of life. The message of this card offers insight into the best way for you to direct your life-sustaining creative flow, avoiding stagnation and damming. Water follows the path of least resistance, carving new ways to get from here to there.

INIPI SPREAD

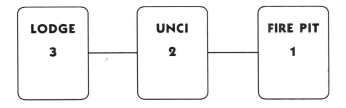

The Inipi spread offers a path of purification and healing. It is a quick and effective way to identify what must be addressed and resolved to bring you back to wholeness, and it offers the guidance to do so.

To heal, one must acknowledge that an imbalance exists. Bring to this spread the willingness to be honest with yourself. Any pain encountered will be passed through as you accept the gifts offered through the subsequent cards.

While in this spread, it is helpful to keep in mind the relationship between the fire pit and the Sun, and between the Lodge and Mother Earth, and to remember Unci, the bridge between the two.

1. The Fire Pit: This card represents that which requires healing. The card you selected will speak to you of imbalance: There is either too much or too little expression of this quality in your life.

2. Unci: Putting into action that which is suggested by this card will realign your body, mind, and spirit into cooperative wholeness, restoring the needed balance to walk your path with grace, upright and strong.

3. The Lodge: Through this card you are given the means to support and sustain your newly healed life. Consider all levels of meaning found in the gift presented to you. Know that as you act upon these ideas you nourish not only yourself but all that enters your life as well.

GRANDFATHER'S BREATH SPREAD

Within the lodge we ask Wakan Tanka to hear our prayers. The heated stones are doused with water, creating great billows of steam that carry the prayers to the sky when the flap door is opened.

The Grandfather's Breath spread allows us to fully

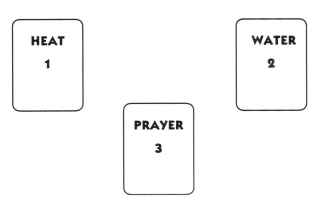

understand the nature of our prayers to Wakan Tanka.
What have you been praying for? Do you understand
your intentions? If answered as you desire, will the good
of all involved be increased? Are you frustrated that you
have recognized no answer?

This spread serves to clarify such issues by opening
the mind and heart, allowing them to blend into the
formlessness of Grandfather's Breath.

Begin by taking a few deep breaths. As you exhale,
release the sense of need and let go of expectation. Inhale
the breath of creation—fulfilling, unrestricted, and light
as air.

1. Heat: The first card is the path of release. We cannot
   take in something new if we are overburdened with
   what is no longer needed. This card suggests what
   will support an effective releasing or, perhaps more
   directly, what to release that we may receive.

2. Water: The second card speaks to our role as creator
   with Wakan Tanka. Sometimes what we desire falls

THE LAKOTA SWEAT LODGE CARDS

into our laps, but usually there is action required from us. We are asked to join with Wakan Tanka, to be the mind, the heart, the arms and legs that create within the world; to satisfy the desires with which we are blessed.

3. Prayer: The third card represents an issue that is unclear or misdirected in your present understanding. This aspect needs to be carried to your Higher Self to be made whole. It needs to be raised up to a new level of light that will allow its true nature to expand you.

GRANDMOTHER'S PATH SPREAD (THE FIREKEEPER'S WALK)

Unci is the Grandmother's Path that is the bridge between the fire and the lodge and on which the energy of Wi travels to Maka to produce new life. The Grandmother's Path spread represents the seven steps the firekeeper follows to carry the heated stone relatives from the transforming fire to the Lodge of rebirth.

You are given seven steps with which to prepare for transformation and rebirth. You are led through the self-examination and exploration necessary for enduring change; you are shown your strength and your support along the Grandmother's Path.

If you have ever been near a large fire, you know the kind of heat it produces. If you have served as a firekeeper, you know, most intimately, that the intensity of the heat is only part of the experience. One who acts as firekeeper must have great respect for the physical and spiritual aspects of the Sacred Fire. The firekeeper is willing to go beyond the arena of comfort, and accepts the challenges and lessons of the Fire with gladness and appreciation. With humble heart, the firekeeper asks to learn what needs to be known for his or her life walk. Begin this spread with the attitude of the firekeeper.

1. The firekeeper has entered the blasting heat of the fire pit and emerges with the very stone that called to be chosen. As she takes the first step along Unci, she freely feels the power she has just encountered. An image surfaces, an image of self in relation to that power.

   This card represents how you see yourself at this time in your life or how you wish you could see yourself. Hear the message of the card with an open, accepting heart, trusting that honesty will guide you along the right path.

2. The firekeeper looks down the path before her to the lodge. Her face is hot and the skin is tight from being in the fire pit; she may wonder if her eyebrows are still there. The stone that called to be carried is a large one. It is heavy, and the lodge is many steps away. All this is felt in the flash of a moment and cast aside. The firekeeper again focuses on the path and the lodge and moves forward.

   Your second step is to understand what is limiting

THE LAKOTA SWEAT LODGE CARDS

you, what is keeping you from moving forward on your path. Is it fear? Is it a belief you didn't realize you carried with you? This card will illuminate that which causes you to hesitate, doubt, or give up. With the gift of this understanding, you may move forward toward your goal undistracted.

3. As the firekeeper walks along Unci to the lodge, a bough of green leaves is used to dust smoldering cinders from the stones. These cinders are of the wood used to build the Sacred Fire and heat the rocks—a vital part of the Inipi ceremony. But cinders within the lodge only cause stinging eyes. The gift of the wood was important earlier, but to take it forward would only cause pain.

    What was once vital to your growth has traveled beyond its time with you and is causing discomfort. This card addresses what you must now leave behind and offers you the best way to do so.

4. The firekeeper is midway between the fire pit and the lodge. She feels part of the sacred pattern of the Inipi and of all power therein. She gracefully lends her strength to the ceremony as she moves forward.

    You are gifted with may strengths. The card chosen for the fourth step represents a strength you are now called to use or develop on your path. Allowing this strength to work for you, lend it to all those within the pattern of your life.

5. The firekeeper now knows she will reach the lodge in a good way. She proceeds forward, feeling the rightness of her steps. This card represents action to

be taken that will facilitate your growth and bring you to the confidence that you will indeed attain your goal—the place of rebirth.

6. As the firekeeper moves forward, the energy from the lodge reaches out in greeting. She feels the support of the gathering spirits as they acknowledge her and honor her service within the ceremony.

   The sixth card tells you of the innumerable sources of support traveling with you as you journey. A spirit gift of acknowledgment and honoring is presented to you. Accept this gift, consciously allowing yourself to be supported.

7. The firekeeper now squats at the door of the lodge, delivering the stone relatives to the seekers within. A ray of sun streams through the dark interior and lights upon one face within. The firekeeper smiles, for the face is her own.

   You have worked hard and honestly on this path of preparation. The card selected here illuminates your vision of yourself in the future. Remember that the future began with your first step.

TREE OF LIFE SPREAD

The Tree of Life spread offers us a path to understanding all aspects of an issue. The spread provides the guidance to effectively bring balance to that situation.

It is important to remember that we are all leaves of the Tree of Life, no more or less vital than any other leaf. We all draw nourishment from the same sap, which feeds

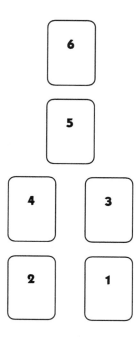

each individual's unique pattern and color, vision and
life. As you use this spread, seek to find that which fos-
ters unity and balance, love and respect.

1. The first card is the beginning place. What is presented here is what you must first give to yourself
   in order to successfully proceed through the spread.
   Does the card suggest love, clarity, seeing both sides,
   or accepting change? Take the time to find the part
   of you to which this card speaks. Accept the gift of
   this insight, feeling the breezes of shifting energy as
   you begin to rebalance yourself.

2. After giving to yourself through the first card, you
   now have the means to give something of value to

others for the development of the situation. This card identifies that which is to be shared. Before interacting with stress, prepare this gift and present it humbly.

3. The third card speaks of the development and expression of your individuality. Bring the gift of this card into your inner world of thought and the outer world of action. The ways you express your truth is as important as the truth itself.

4. Meeting another's individuality or your own inner conflict can produce tension. The card speaks of the awareness you require to successfully and respectfully work toward balance.

5. The fifth card describes how to enlarge upon the fourth card by offering you insight into areas you need to develop or strengthen in order to walk in balance in the world. The issue you have presented to the cards has its larger component in the world. Receiving this gift now allows you to share your new insights with the entire Tree.

6. The sixth and final card is the outcome of the path taken through the preceding cards. It ultimately speaks of your role as one who seeks to restore balance and to honor all life.

MORNING STAR SPREAD

At the top of the Inipi lodge, the white willow poles cross, forming an eight-pointed star. Each point represents one of the morning stars, the planets that revolve

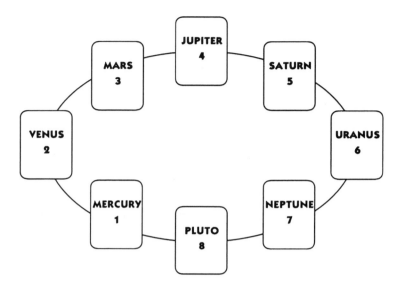

with Maka around the sun, and reflect the light of Wi with soft illumination.

Each of these luminaries shines light on an aspect of your being. You can use the Morning Star spread to illuminate your many aspects within a particular issue or situation or to look at yourself as you are today, in more general terms.

1. Mercury: The first card reflects how you communicate with the world. Is the reflection one that pleases you, or does it indicate the need for development in some way?

2. Venus: The second card reflects your values and where you direct your love. Is the message an accurate image of your conscious living? Is the message a surprise to you? If so, it is time to delve below the

surface to find the true love hidden beneath the apparent one and energize it.

3. Mars: The third card reflects how you engage your energies with the world around you. Does the message of this card speak of balance, or does it call for development or refinement?

4. Jupiter: The fourth card reflects how you relate to opportunities and areas of potential growth. Does this card reflect the truth of your spirit, or is it clouded in some way?

5. Saturn: The fifth card reflects how you address self-preservation. Does it reflect the strength that has brought you this far, alive and willing to learn more, or does it reflect some dimmer light?

6. Uranus: The sixth card reflects how you deal with change or disruption. Does it reflect a soul centered in Wakan Tanka or one that is at the mercy of any gravitational pull?

7. Neptune: The seventh card reflects your reception to inspiration. Are you able to perceive creative images in the watery palette of your mind, or do you find yourself immersed in confused and illusory patterns?

8. Pluto: The eighth and last card reflects the outcome by illuminating the unconscious path shown to be alive in your steps. Are you in rhythm with your own steps, or is there a side of you that is yet to be understood?

PART I

THE SIXTEEN
GREAT MYSTERIES

0

WAKAN TANKA

GREAT SPIRIT

The Source

*We, the servants of Wakan Tanka, say to you:
The Creator, the Beginning and End of your seeking,
speaks to you every moment of your existence.*

*The Creator asks of you one thing only: Open
your heart, and all that you seek will follow.*

TRADITION

Wakan Tanka is the Great Spirit, the Great Mystery, the Grandfather and Creator of all things. Wakan Tanka has always been and will always be.

Wakan Tanka is All That Is. The Gods, everything created, the act of creation itself—these are aspects of the Great Spirit, the One; and the One is *Wakan,* Holy.

Anything that has birth must have a death. The Spirit is not born but given to one at birth, and it is Wakan. Therefore one's Spirit will never die.

THE CARD

You are being reminded that within you is the source of all your peace and joy. You have unlimited opportunities and capabilities to create that which is for your highest good and the good of all. Wakan Tanka is within all things and is at the center of all life. The pathway to your center is the pathway to your inner peace. You can find your peace in the recognition of your connection and oneness with Wakan Tanka and all the creative powers of the universe. Honor the Creator within, and create the path that is right for you. But first walk the path back to the self, back to Wakan Tanka and all that is sacred.

MEDITATION

Great Spirit, guide me in the way of the Open Heart, that I may know you through all moments, in all life.

1

WI

SUN

Personal Power

I am the embodiment of the Source of All Being.
I am all, create all, and devour all.
I am the manifestation of all that is your Creator,
*   Wakan Tanka, the Great Mystery.*
You seek from me words to enlighten.
I live beyond words.
Look at me. Feel me. Experience me.
There is the knowledge you seek.
I am the Light.

TRADITION

According to Lakota tradition, the Creator, Wakan Tanka, was alone in an endless, timeless place. He decided to create from himself Spirit forces through which He would create the universe. In course, He created the Sixteen Mysteries. The first created was Wi, who, from pure Spirit, became the elemental energy of Light and Life, the teacher and sustainer. Wi was transformed into the Sun, with the power to provide the energy for Earth to produce the substance of Life.

THE CARD

You are on the road to becoming, accepting, and acknowledging the power within. The Sun lights your way, making your direction clear, allowing you to see your power. It is time to express your personal power by using your inner gifts. Direct your energy, and you will achieve what you set out to achieve. You may want to sit in the sun, letting its radiance and warmth encircle you with power and strength. Let the sun's light help you gain the confidence you need. Recognize the inner light, the inner radiance, in order to illuminate your personal vision for the future. You will find that once the vision is clear, your power is at hand.

MEDITATION

The energy of the Sun meets with my own and awakens new understandings. I open to the fire, the diversity, the harmony of life.

2

SKAN

MOTION

Manifestation

I am the eternal Now of Creation, that which existed before the creation of Time. I am that through which time moves. Through me, you are given the gifts of experience, reflection, and hope, that these may lead you to know yourself:

To know yourself as creator and created.

To know yourself within the fabric of All That Is.

To know yourself, ultimately, to be no greater than a speck of dust and no less than the God you seek.

TRADITION

Skan, the second spirit set forth from Wakan Tanka, became the Motion of all things. Skan set the stars and planets moving on their paths and released the winds to travel across the universe.

Skan enters the body with the spirit and sets in motion the breath and blood of new life.

All that is created is in motion. The seas, the clouds, the trees, and all that live within and upon the earth move in a dance to the radiance of the One who created all things—Wakan Tanka.

THE CARD

You have the ability to use your inner power of focused thought to attract what you want in your life. Assuredly, the Creator within you will move, through clear and directed thought, to attain the outcome you desire. It's all in your thought process and belief system. Dispel those thoughts that limit you and hold you back. Concentrate on what you wish to create in your life, and allow that which is for your highest good. Treat these blessings you desire as if they are already being directed toward you, and they will appear in your life. Try to make them happen, and you'll be waiting a long time.

MEDITATION

I rejoice in the motion of my body, in the freedom found in movement through time, space, and experience.

3

MAKA

MOTHER EARTH

Birth

I live that you may live.

In the dream time of Creation, I brought forth the womb for mankind and all his brothers. I represent the form of the woman's body. I nourish all to whom I give birth. You, child, are as dear to me as the Elk that roam the forest glade and the Trees that grow upon my body. I speak to you of abiding Love, of sustaining nourishment, of endless rounds of seasons and change.

I give you the gift of being yourself, being creative through your own individual expression. And as a loving mother, I endure the separation and loss of my children, knowing that even as they leave me and denounce me, they are returning to me.

I am a place of rest where you are known in all your aspects. I am your home.

I am she who is your own Heart of hearts. I am creator of life upon this plane. With the energy of the Sun in Motion, I create the Passion that manifests.

Know that I am pleased with my children as they remember their origins and the wisdom of my heart, which is your own.

TRADITION

The third Spirit to emerge from Wakan Tanka was Maka, who took the form of Earth. Maka is the spirit and essence of feminine energy, the source and substance of life. She is the spirit of all that gives forth and sustains life on earth. In Lakota tradition, Wakan Tanka took all the colors of light and, putting them together, created the sacred brown of the Earth Mother. Skan, the Spirit of Motion, blew water onto the earth to create the oceans and seas. And Inyan, Spirit of Equilibrium, came as stone to support the earth, holding her together. Lakotas say "Maka-say-elo"—all things upon this earth are endless.

THE CARD

In the near future you may find yourself giving birth to a new idea, beginning a new enterprise, or starting your life anew in some way. You may have already begun this process. Embrace this new birth by releasing the images and symbols of the past and by accepting the changes that come. Courageously step forth from the safety of the womb into the light of a new day. You can make the changes that you've been wanting to make in your life. Stand on the Earth and feel her support and energy giving you strength. Learn from your Earth Mother. Take your new endeavors out into the world and allow them to bear fruit.

MEDITATION

I open to the feminine within me and surrounding me and find the creativity and support I seek.

4

INYAN

STONE

Support

I am the foundation of the material world. I am the sustainer of the manifest. I am the bones of your Mother. I am the strength upon which you walk upright, that you may raise your arms to the Father above you.

You perceive not the life within me, for I move in such slow rhythm it appears to you as stillness. Yet as you walk upon me, your balance is maintained, allowing wisdom to take root in your conscious mind. I gift you the low notes heard only in your dreams. I allow you to learn your own equilibrium through knowledge of mine. Your Mother Earth is gentle: When you fall upon her, she kisses you; when you fall upon me, you feel pain. You remember to walk with care. You remember balance.

You may call to me to speak to you of my ancient tales of life on this planet, for I have been here throughout Creation. I am truly your Grandfather.

TRADITION

Inyan, the fourth creation of Wakan Tanka, is the force of equilibrium. On earth, Inyan is stone, the foundation and support of the body of Maka, Mother Earth.

All stones in your path are alive. The rock, the mountain, and all minerals are the material body of Inyan. Inyan Ska, the quartz crystal, lives and grows within the dark interior of the earth and, carrying this dark energy, becomes clear.

THE CARD

Inyan is telling you to look at your foundation and take steps to create balance in your life. What do you need to bring into your life to be more emotionally balanced? Use the wisdom of the stone to bring harmony to your surroundings. The stresses in your life may be tilting your sense of balance. Examine the influences that create stress and find ways to minimize them. Determine your priorities and relax some of the pressures you've placed on yourself. Handle those situations facing you with diplomacy, considering the pros and cons, so you can stand more solidly when making decisions.

MEDITATION

I allow the strength and stability that already resides within me to awaken and rise through my being and be known to me.

5

HANWI

MOON

Reflection

I am the subtle yet powerful force of cycles upon
your planet and body. I shift the tides, and I shift
your moods and your receptivity.

I am a light that shines in the darkness, for never,
dear one, are you without the guidance of All That
Is Life. When I shine upon you as you sleep, I draw
you into the misty reflections of all that I have seen.

I quicken change and motion. I relieve headaches
with the coolness of my light. I work with my sis-

*ters of the sea in rhythmic respirations of life. When
I am hidden from you, I offer you the opportunity to
find within yourself the reflection of Spirit.*

TRADITION

In the Lakota story of creation, Maka, Mother Earth,
traveled around Wi, Sun, who warmed and lighted but
half her body. Maka asked Wi to warm the side that was
cold and dark. Wi created from himself Hanwi, Moon,
and placed her on the far side of the Earth so that the
Sun's light, reflected, would comfort and illumine the
Earth's dark side.

Han is "darkness," *wi* is "sun." *Hanwi* is the "night
sun." Hanwi ceremonies in darkness as she crosses the
night sky. Certain ceremonies and rituals are performed
with the night energies. The energies of darkness and the
energies of light complement each other. Through the
light of the sun and the light of the moon, Wakan Tanka
gives us the sacred Balance of Energies.

THE CARD

We live in a world of cycles that offer opportunities for
reflection, understanding, and growth. Drawing the card
of Hanwi suggests that these cycles must be acknowledged and the gifts accepted. We cannot sustain one
mood, one way of perceiving, one action only, throughout
our lives or even throughout our day.

Receive the rhythmic balancing changes within you
and those around you with grace. Reflect on the relief
from stress, on the freedom of expression, and on security

in the future given by these cycles. Accept Spirit as the
soft illumination as well as the bold sun.

MEDITATION

I open to the grace of Beauty, the Light of Spirit shin-
ing in all Creation.

6

TATE
WIND
Change

I am born of the imminent Motion of Creation. I am all that was, is, and will be. I am the blessed breath of the One Who Loves you. I am the necessity of motion manifest in your world. I give you the experience of time—of past, present, and future. I share my breath with all Earth's children. I can be gentle and caressing; I can bring destruction. I am he who sees to it that no creation begotten of man lives forever, for this is against the Law of my Father,

Skan, who says that these children must learn from experience, from change, internal and external, until the knowledge of his origin is all that is left to know.

But I need not be harsh with you, dear one. Hear the message in my soft voice. Then I need not become so loud but for my own exuberance.

I have much to tell you, for I travel far and wide, high and low. I swirl in eddies over the seas and rise high unto our Father and return again to the surface of the earth with messages for you.

TRADITION

Skan, the Spirit of Motion, created Tate. Tate, Wind, began to blow across the earth carrying the seed of the Life Force, blowing it into the waiting human, the waiting plant. The force of Tate is carried within the seed and passed down through the generations.

THE CARD

Consider stirring things up and making some major changes in your life. The wind carries seeds to their new place of growth, and the changes that you make loosen the topsoil, allowing you to cultivate the new ground to which you have been carried. There are times when major changes are called for; other times a slight adjustment is beneficial. Whether you make a change in diet, move the furniture, or change your place of residence or your career, it is up to you to look within to find the shift appropriate for you. So, if there is a life change you have been avoiding, it is now time to take steps to cultivate that change.

MEDITATION

I trust the deep promptings of self that guide me through change.

7

UNK

SATISFACTION & PASSION

To Walk in Balance

When you live with Passion, you are receiving the full gift of life. I excite all the systems of your being. All your senses become acutely aware.

The full current of your life surges toward the object of your passion, be it another human, a work of art, an idea or principle.

I am created by Maka, Mother Earth. In Motion with the Sun, the very Law of Life is satisfied, for I am experience in all its delicious splendor. There is no line between passion and satisfaction, for only in passion is the life-urge fulfilled.

TRADITION

Maka, Mother Earth, created Unk to feed her children the passion and satisfaction of life. Unk is the yearning and delight between lovers, between a person and a beloved activity or thing, between a person and spiritual understanding. The balance inherent in passion is the balance among the mental, physical, and spiritual needs we must satisfy in order to feel whole.

THE CARD

Passion is the stimulant, a powerful driving force that allows us to feel the essence of life. We are capable of experiencing and expressing intense emotions and responses. Allow the flow of passion in your life. When you are experiencing the passion, you are fully experiencing the moment. Don't deny one of life's most precious gifts. Determine where your passion lies, and embrace that aspect of your life. Acknowledge and accept your true feelings as they arise, and let the enthusiasm generated help you walk in balance with your emotions.

MEDITATION

I open to my passion, and life becomes ever more beautiful, ever more satisfying. I allow my passions life and find myself in joy.

8

WAKINYAN

THUNDERBEINGS

Energy

To know me, know the storms I bring, storms that cut like a knife through the building heat of day. Know the raw power of the Lightning that flashes and sears. Know the sound of my voice as I call out what I am charged to do.

I am created from Stone. In his wisdom, Inyan sent me forth into the world to oversee the caretakers of Earth, to assist them in their role. I am like no human. I am electric energy, and I course through all things. My current cleanses and destroys. My great wings bring sudden and terrible winds. The raw energy from my eye changes the vision of a human.

TRADITION

Inyan, Spirit of the Stone, created Wakinyan, who became the Thunderbeings, the force of electricity on the earth. Wakinyan is the spirit who controls the essence of the clouds, the motion of hurricanes, tornadoes, and storms. In the language of the Lakota, *wa* is the flying of the snow and *inyan* is stone. Wakinyan is the physical electricity that comes from the water, the earth, and the air, building up to create thunder and lightning.

Thunderbeings, represented as the Thunderbird, are honored by many tribes. Wakinyan flies without eyes, without ears, without mouth, without nose. Even in visions, no one can behold Wakinyan whole. Those to whom he comes in dreams become *heyoka*, sacred clowns who do everything backward. Wakinyan is the force of truth: He strikes down anyone who lies while holding the Sacred Pipe. His spirit-eye opens with the flash of lightning and the sound of thunder.

THE CARD

Allow your natural polarities to help direct you in your walk of life. You have choices about how to conduct your energies and where to channel them. Using your skills, let your unique electricity flow in the direction of the highest good. Be conscious of the direction in which you cast your lightning bolts; take care not to throw them in a haphazard manner. Careless use of energy might mean wasting this personal dynamic on projects irrelevant to your inner self. When energies are not wisely conserved but are short-circuited, a storm brews within, and you are more likely to throw your thunderbolts without control. There is an endless supply of energy. Wakinyan generates all that you need. Ask for the guidance to galvanize your attention, and get ready to throw your thunderbolts before you to help illuminate your next steps.

MEDITATION

Through the single Eye of Spirit, my path becomes clear and my energy becomes focused and effective.

9

TATANKA OYATE
THE BISON NATION/MAN
Attainment

I am here: Spirit of the Bison Nation, Spirit of the creation of Humanity. I saw fit to put upon the Earth one who would live differently from his brothers, yet not; one who would join the spirits of all beings, yet remain intact. I am present in this day among you. I seek recognition from you. I am the very Essence of animal/human kinship. I am that you may say, Aho Mitakuye Oyasin.

TRADITION

The ninth Great Mystery is the creation of humankind on the earth. The name *Tatanka* does not convey the true spiritual immanence attached to the bison. The ancient name *Pté* meant "the people," "realizing the highest form," and *Tatanka Pté*, "the people of the bison," signifies the interrelationship of the bison with the people who used every part of the great beast for sustenance. The White Buffalo Calf Woman, Pté San Wi, is the prophet who came to teach the sacred ways to the people; her gifts of the Sacred Pipe and its ceremony are also derived from the spiritual energy of the buffalo.

The sacred song says: "A Bison Nation is walking, A Bison Nation is walking. . . . I give you this beautiful earth, and upon it you shall live and multiply. I give you the Sacred Pipe, and with it you shall come to the center of the earth. All that you ask shall be given to you."

THE CARD

Your past action and the faith you have shown have led you to the attainment of your higher goal. You will be experiencing this on both the physical and spiritual levels. Remember to give thanks for all that you attain and to congratulate yourself for a job well done and for your patience and perseverance.

If you have not yet achieved the fruits of your labor, you are either being asked to use your skills and gifts more fully or to keep faith and be patient—success is on its way. There is much to accomplish in life, and it is all waiting for your approach, one step at a time.

MEDITATION

I know myself within the abundance and diversity of
life upon the Earth and celebrate our kinship.

10

TOB TOB

BEAR

Wisdom

Bear I am. Bear I be. Eternal as all forces of Nature. I am the guardian of all my children, the four-leggeds of the earth. I sit in silence and observe. I sit in silence, in the dark of my den, and communicate with our Mother Earth. I speak when I know what must be said. I act when I know what must be done. When I speak and when I act, all within great distances know that I have done so, for when I speak and when I act, it is a force that sets things right.

TRADITION

As humanity expanded beyond instinctual knowing, the need for protection and wisdom had to take a new form. *Tob* means "four." *Tob Tob* means "four times four," the expanding progression, the wisdom of four-legged animals, extending to the extremes of the Four Directions, communicated by the Four Winds. Tob Tob is the interrelatedness of the individual within the matrix of creation, the personal truth within the truth of the family, within the truth of the tribe, the nation, the world, the universe. Through the wisdom of Tob Tob, Bear, we come to recognize what is right for us as individuals. Bear knows what plants and herbs to dig for sustenance, when to fight and when to hibernate.

THE CARD

You are being asked to use the divine wisdom that is within each of us to reach for that which is for your highest good. Wisdom is the ability to see the connection of all life and to accept all things as they are. That includes fully accepting yourself in any given moment. Wisdom links the intuitive feelings with the fact and information known to the mind. When you act from a place of wisdom, you allow guidance, opening yourself to the information provided by the universe. Avoid the assumption that every opportunity is a message from the universe urging an action you should take. You have choice. Use your inner wisdom to determine if it's the right time and opportunity for you. Act upon what you feel as well as what you know.

MEDITATION

I give myself time to be separate and silent, allowing deep and guided knowing to emerge.

11
WANI

THE FOUR DIRECTIONS

Lessons

*I am the wind that travels from the Four
Directions, carrying and depositing the seeds of life.
Like the snow, my seed disappears into the earth
only to reappear in a new form.*

*I am the circle of your consciousness, which
grows and expands, through experience, to the place
of Beauty, the place where all life is known to be
celebration and joy.*

I am the cry of the newborn, who feels the first pangs of separation and wholeness. I am the cry of all life that comes into awareness of this mystery.

My friends, do not stop that which is growing. Allow the garden of life to give of its gifts to you in all forms even unto death, which is no ending but a continuation of the Circle of Life.

TRADITION

Tate, Wind, sent his sons to create the four Cardinal Points to the west, north, east, and south. Wani has a deep spiritual meaning in Lakota teachings. *Wa* means "snow" and *ni* means "life," as if to say, "I am alive now." The snow melts into the earth, helping all to live; its seasonal passing nourishes the Circle of Life. The dimensions of space and time established by the Four Directions are the source of harmony and proportion in the physical world—the means by which our senses teach us the beauty of creation. Life is so beautiful, we must learn to walk with life in a beautiful way.

THE CARD

Each of the Four Directions has its own lessons to teach us, some difficult, some immediately clear. There are those that take a long time to learn, others that suddenly erupt, creating upheaval in our lives. There are important lessons that seem baffling, elusive. At any moment, a new lesson may be presenting itself to us, but we are not always aware of the gifts being offered.

Awaken to the lessons in your life. Open your eyes

and take in the messages coming to you from all directions. Relax into the center of the four-cornered circle, and allow the teachings to surround and uplift you, taking you forward into new territory. Although at times you may feel as if you are being pulled into a tailspin, or carried without support, trust and know that the lessons you need are always presented when you are ready. Ask for the direction and help you need.

MEDITATION

The seed of life brought me forth and resides within me. I create a fertile home for this seed through a life rich in love, beauty, and creativity.

12

YUM

THE WHIRLWIND

Love

As your blood flows through your veins, as the waters rush upon the earth, so am I. I am the beauty in a newborn's face. I am the intense yellow of the jonquil. I am the joy between two lovers. I am laughter, I am elation.

My dance stirs all creation. The game of the whirlwind catches up everything, sets everything down on different ground, changed by the time spent with me.

I am born upon this earth in female form. I find my home in the endless flow of Love through all forms, the timeless circles of swirling waters.

TRADITION

Skan, Motion, and Hanwi, Moon, created from themselves the Spirit called Yum, or Yumeni Wi—the most beautiful of all God's creations. Friction arose between Hanwi and Yum, and Yum was put apart in a place of honor. She was made Goddess of the Sea, Goddess of Love, Goddess of Sport, Goddess of Games. Her domain lies within the sea and all bodies of water. Her force governs all living things and presides in the love people feel.

She symbolizes all that moves in circles: the whirlwind, the cycles of the seasons and of life, the planets, the stars.

THE CARD

Be conscious of the flow of love. Do you freely allow love into your life? Do you give love with ease? Awaken the love within you so that you can pour waves of loving energy into the world. Let the tenderness of love embrace you, surround you, and fill you, expanding your nature. Walk out into the world newly expanded, radiating gentle love, offering unity to all you meet. Share your love with the people and objects involved in all your actions.

Bring love and awareness to every task, so that you perform it with balance and harmony. Look at the tasks that you have avoided, and practice performing them with love. Recognize the difference in how the work affects you; see the benefits. Look at problematic personal relationships that cause tension. Take a chance—love the difficult individual, and feel fear and tension dissipate.

MEDITATION

I provide myself the space to connect with the endless flow of loving energy that sustains me. Thus may I discover the flow of love that surrounds me.

13

NIYAN

SPIRIT OF MAN

Higher Self

I speak to you from inside yourself. I am your-self. I am that in you that knows that I am of the Creator. I am that in you that knows I am eternal. I am that in you that sees the Creator in all things. I am that in you that speaks of Truth. I am your own Self. I am the navigator through experience. I am you—I am your brother, and your mother, and each two-legged who walks this earth.

TRADITION

Wakan Tanka created Niyan, the Human Spirit, so that people would understand their life and death. The Creator said, "I will give you a Spirit and you will know that life is nothing but circles, the Universal Circle, a circle without end. The Spirit is eternal and never stops traveling the Circle of Life.

"The body I give you does not belong to you. It belongs to Me, who created all things. The body I give you belongs to the Earth Mother and it shall return to her. When your life ends, your body will return to the Earth and your Spirit will go on to the Spirit World."

THE CARD

Our spirit is that which connects us to the eternal, to our source, and to all things. Acknowledge your essential identity—your Higher Self. You have the resources within to handle all situations, to make all decisions, to answer all questions. It is easy for us to lose sight of this; often we look outward for answers and direction, and accept influences that may not be suited for us.

Remember to seek guidance within, and do so with patience and trust. Your inborn support and guidance are there at all times. Your answer will come through symbols and messages best suited to your own perceptions— through dreams, a chance meeting, a quotation in a book, or by any number of paths. Some answers come immediately, some overnight, others may be received at some time in the future—only when you've reached the level of wisdom or experience to truly understand the full range of the matter in question. Whatever the time frame or method, it is your role to trust, without preconceptions, that guidance will be provided.

MEDITATION
I acknowledge the Truth that lives in my being. Through experience I learn to trust my inner knowing and honor the whole of my being.

14

NAGI

GHOST

Shadow Self

I am the one you choose not to see. I am caught, trapped, unnoticed, unable to change because I am without recognition. I am unloved and unnurtured because I am unseen. I am powerless to move on without your help. Bring me into the World of Light with your attention. Guide me on my path. Love me.

TRADITION

In Lakota tradition, the ghost is the shadow of a human. Between the physical world and the Spirit World is another circle, an intermediate world for those who have not lived in the world according to the Laws of Spirit. There are those who have used and abused for personal gain, those who have taken their own life or the life of another. These spirits do not enter the Spirit World. They are destined to walk the endless circle of time. The only way they can go beyond the Circle of the Ghost is by the prayers and offerings of the living. The Spirit World is for those who have lived according to the ways of the Creator: harmony, balance, one mind, one prayer.

THE CARD

Whatever is not in balance cannot effectively take part in the physical or spiritual worlds. There are ghostlike, unbalanced aspects of our own lives that we don't notice, no matter how clearly these shadows of ourselves can be seen by others. How do other people view you? How does this view differ from your own image of yourself?

It no longer serves you to push the shadow aside. Embrace your Shadow Self and acknowledge its existence, providing these personal traits with a home in your consciousness. You may find that some disregarded traits have been giving you support and strength.

MEDITATION

I welcome all aspects of my life into the Light of Consciousness for recognition and healing. I claim my lost selves with love and restore my internal harmony.

15

SICUN

INTELLECT

Discernment

I am the Creator's gift to humanity. I separate humanity's path from all other paths in creation. As with all gifts, I am to be received by you with gratitude and used with wisdom. Through me, a human is changed from a blind follower of unknown laws to a decision maker. This requires acknowledgment of vast stimuli on a conscious and unconscious level. This requires an internal faith in this mechanism. This requires responsibility for actions

taken. I am that which allows for this process, which allows for integration of Spirit and mind. I enable you to evaluate and choose. Use me as I have been intentioned—with compassion.

TRADITION

As humanity grew into its role as caretaker of the earth, the Great Spirit gave humans intellect and the knowledge of right and wrong. In modern times, the balance of intellect and intuition has been lost. This imbalance has separated us from our sisters and brothers, the four-leggeds, the winged ones, those that crawl, and those that swim. It has separated us from the elements and from the Earth Mother.

Using intellect in rhythm with the heartbeat of the Earth Mother is to walk in balance.

THE CARD

You have been given the great power to reason and the capacity for knowledge and understanding. Your intellect provides you with judgment, rational thinking, and the ability to handle new and difficult situations. This is a gentle reminder to use it wisely.

Let your mind provide you with the helpful information you need at any given moment, but be wary of getting caught up in the thinking process for its sake alone. Balance your ability to learn and reason with your ability to feel and express emotion. You have been given the power of the mind; remember to give your heart equal time. Use your intellect to mesh thought and feeling as you walk your path. Both are necessary to keep you on track; let them carry you as a team. Sometimes your heart will propel you and your mind will steer you along your course; other times it will be your curiosity that drives you and your heart that keeps you from straying. It is your privilege to discern when to be guided by your intellect and when to let your heart direct your way. One without the other will never secure your best interests.

MEDITATION

I honor my gift of intellect, allowing the support and balance of intuition. I accept responsibility for my decisions and aim always to learn the way of balance.

16

YUMENI WHOUHA

THE MATERIAL

Abundance

Believe that you are provided for, for it is so.
Our Father created me that you may know this. As
you come to trust in yourself, you will know me as
one who leads you through knowledge of Giving
and Receiving. Our Creator wishes you to fill your
stomach and keep your body warm. Wakan Tanka
wishes that you feast at the appointed times. He
also wishes you to care and share among your-
selves, that you work in harmony with Tate. Know

that all things of the material world are passing.
Receive in gratitude and release in joy.

TRADITION

The Creator gave humanity the knowledge of the material gifts of life: tools to hunt and forage, clothes for warmth and expression, shelter from the elements and for gathering together. Thus was given all that was necessary for survival.

In Lakota tradition, a person's wealth is measured not by what one possesses but by what one gives away. A person understands that cycles of change—times of scarcity and times of abundance—are natural to this world and that the Great Spirit provides all that is, for all the people. The flow of material possessions through our hands is known to be from the bounty of the Creator, to be blessed and appreciated and released into the cycles established by the Great Spirit.

THE CARD

Abundance is yours. Everything you need to sustain life has been provided for you. It is all there for you, once you accept it. It is your responsibility to allow the abundance into your life. You must become centered and balanced in the material world by comfortably giving and receiving. Give thanks for all that is provided to you and be able to release that which has been received. We all share the abundance of the earth.

Beware of the importance you place on your material possessions. Release your hold on your belongings and relinquish your fears of scarcity; an impoverished attitude brings forth poverty, while the acceptance of abundance allows for abundance. Lighten your load and begin to give some of your belongings away. Let them go.

Your sense of abundance need not be limited to financial prosperity and material possessions. We are provided with a true wealth of love, companionship, teachings, guidance, and nourishment—riches we have only to accept.

MEDITATION

I acknowledge with gratitude the flow of God's abundance through my life.

PART II

THE EIGHT
SUPERNATURALS

17

ANOGETE

WOMAN WITH TWO FACES

Duality

You find me so hard to understand that I exist in your world as one entity. In this world you most easily perceive as linear is another dimension: polarity. I am one, not two. I am the unseen and the seen, the unspoken and the spoken, the chaos and the very order of Nature. Because you sense me but cannot see me, you fear me and think me a perver-

*sion. But truly, it is your fear that perverts, for I am
as natural to the fabric of your world as the sun
that continues to shine above the dark thunder
clouds. When you understand me, I no longer seem
a twisted thing. Rather, you understand that I am
the limit of experience in your world.*
And why else are you here?

TRADITION

Anogete is a supernatural aspect of Hanwi, Moon. The
face of Anogete is half beautiful and half hideous. Her
role is to assist humans in finding their way through perceived negativity to the One who exists behind and within the duality of good and bad, light and dark, positive
and negative, male and female.

THE CARD

There is duality in all things: the positive and the negative, the dark and light, the internal and external, and the
masculine and feminine aspects of all life. Take time to
look at both sides of all situations so you can see the
whole picture. What is being presented to you is only one
of the two faces, the most easily perceived. Rather than
seeing that which you expect, open your perspective to
see the side that's been blocked from view. The two sides
exist simultaneously within the whole. Give them equal
time and weight. Balance your perception. If you have
only seen the positive, allow the negative to appear, and
accept its existence without dismissing it.

MEDITATION

Releasing fear and judgment, I open my perceptions to wholeness, to One.

18

IKTOMI

SPIDER

Fear of the Unseen

I am like a whisper. You do not see me. I come on tiptoe from dark places. I move quickly and can almost fly. Can't you see that I am magic? Yet when I step within your home or upon your skin—ha! What a ruckus ensues! One would think a giant monster had appeared to you. Sometimes I will bite you—perhaps because you deserve it, perhaps because I like to tease. You know, I go about build-

ing webs and catching things to eat without much thought of you. But when we meet, I know what you feel; and if it is fear, then you are my prey.

TRADITION

Iktomi is the Supernatural Spirit who deceives everyone—or at least tries. There are many stories of Iktomi changing himself into a human in order to fool everyone, but he always makes a mistake, revealing his true nature. He brings laughter through his foolish acts. He is like a human who tries to be what he cannot be.

As the deceiver, building webs that snare, Iktomi weaves the threads of your fear. He teaches us to avoid creating a web of deception that will only ensnare us and those we love.

THE CARD

You may find yourself trapped in the web of fear. Some of our anxieties cannot be explained or even connected to anything in particular. Just the fear of getting caught in an unseen web can immobilize us.

You are not a victim entangled in a web but someone who can choose to detach yourself from fear by recognizing and renouncing it. You can step back and become an observer of your own life, looking at the entire pattern rather than the single strand of fear. When this invisible fear seems to block your path, you will find that if you concentrate on the goals before you, you can walk through the fear to the other side.

MEDITATION

Using the courage gifted to me by my Creator, I walk through my fears with honesty and integrity.

19

KANKA

OLD WOMAN SORCERESS

Dreams

I am so old. I know Everything. See me as I sit and rock to and fro, babbling of all I know. For all time, this is so. The powers I have are endless. I could point to you now and change you into a toad, but I choose not to. In your dreams, I am the wise old woman who guides you. I am the young, powerful sorceress who sets your mind spinning.

I am so old. I tell you, I know Everything. You

may be so foolish as to believe me. Understand this: Not all vision reveals pure Being. But all visions have something for you to know. Know that I am fond of tricks.

TRADITION

Kanka, the sorceress, who appears as an old woman or witch, is a Supernatural Spirit who transforms. She is the energy of the positive and negative transmuting into each other. It was she who brought the sacred teachings of the Inipi ceremony to the people, that they might purify themselves and restore life.

Kanka is also called "the Holy Veins of the Nation," for she protects the Teachings, "the Blood of the Nation," through the generations. The Way of the Teachings is "the Red Road."

THE CARD

Spend time examining dreams—answers and guidance can be found in the imagery. Dreams indicate communication from your higher, inner self—messages to guide your personal development. Look within the symbols for the hidden messages and lessons. They are important intelligence for self-exploration and understanding.

MEDITATION

I seek the teachings that guide me through all of life's experiences. I use my gift of discernment to unlock the truth.

20

KSA
GODDESS OF WATER
Uncover

In my mother before me was created the beauty of love. As her child, I am always in turmoil until I present myself to her and her beauty—her love soothes me. I sleep sometimes in the depth of my home, far from all others but my mother, and dream the visions of Skan. I awaken restless and troubled, until I turn to her again and all becomes beauty. I hide myself near the breast of Maka and listen to her heartbeat, which unites us all.

I give to you the power of transforming emotions. Bring your troubles to Yum, to Love, through me, for I have her ear and I know your turmoil. Yum, the beloved of Skan, cannot deny you the needed perspective.

TRADITION

Skan, Motion, and Hanwi, Moon, created for themselves the spirit called Yum, The Whirlwind. Yum split from herself the Supernatural Ksa, Goddess of Water. *Ksa* means "to cut from oneself," to transplant. This split allows Yum to be wholly positive.

Ksa, the negative side of the Goddess Yum, is the goddess of water and the seas. She acts with Ibom, the negative male energy, creating storms and destruction. They are the ultimate balancers.

THE CARD

As we flow through life, we must deal with many issues. Although there are times we feel as if we are deep in turbulent waters, our most significant concerns only truly rise to the surface when we are ready to face them. Allow them to surface as they will. These concerns may have been hidden from view, too heavy to rise. Once they've surfaced, however, they are lighter, easier to face, and in a place where they can be resolved. As your issues float, uncovered, they are illuminated. Stand back to get a clearer picture—do not allow yourself to become immersed with them. Ask yourself what reasons there are for these issues to appear in your life. How have they benefitted you in the past, and how would you like to see them benefit you in the future? Take the opportunity to confront them now rather than allow them to sink into the deep waters of your consciousness, only to be brought to the surface once again in the future.

MEDITATION

As turbulence appears in my life, I search for the love present in all circumstances. From this perspective, I view the way of positive resolution.

21

WAZI

OLD MAN SORCERER OF THE NORTH

Resolution

I move always with a smile, and I always am moving. I am fond of you humans, and so I travel always, to know what is happening among you. I am old, yes; but I am not aged. I suffer no ailments, no hesitation. I bring you the wisdom of my source, the Vitalizers of the North, the strength of sure knowledge.

TRADITION

Wazi, a Supernatural Spirit, is known as the Old Man, the Sorcerer of the North. He is known in the form of the clouds that blow from the north, bringing the snows and rains that vitalize.

THE CARD

You are on the road to resolving an issue in your life. Decisions will be made regarding this issue, and you will be able to move toward a successful conclusion with confidence and clarity. The doubts that have cluttered your mind in the past will begin to dissolve, allowing you to make firm decisions without being pulled in two directions. As you resolve all conflict in this area, you become lighter, released from the weight of the issue. Let your Higher Self guide you, and you will be able to move past resolution.

MEDITATION

I honor the essence of the North, the Vitalizers. I honor the place of Wisdom within and without.

22

TOB TOB

EIGHT DIRECTIONS
OF THE WIND

Self-protection

I am here from long ago when human beings chose to pursue a path separate from that of the brothers and sisters, the four-leggeds, and the relatives that swim and fly. No longer would you humans live the life of instinctual knowing. That which you wished to know had expanded beyond that place. No longer would you talk with your relatives and be protected.

So I came to you to offer a new protection, in order that you may survive: the wisdom of change. I come from the Four Directions and the four points between, bringing you an opportunity to understand your unique soul. Your life is like no other's life, your needs are like no other's needs. I bring you the wisdom of knowing what to change, how to change, into what to change, that you may receive the gifts of Wani and celebrate your life.

TRADITION

Tob Tob of the Sixteen Great Mysteries split its personality so that it was all positive and Tob Tob the Supernatural became the force of the negative. The four points between, the four negative directions of the wind, carry personal challenges to those in its path. They are the Northwest, the Northeast, the Southeast, and the Southwest. People in the north call these winds the Chinook winds. In the south they are called the Santa Anas. Tob Tob the Supernatural flies with the wind from the sea, across the desert, the mountains, the plains, and is the unseen force that comes with these winds, affecting the motion of life.

THE CARD

You are being asked to look at your safety and protection, to take steps to protect yourself from internal and external interference while keeping your self-esteem intact. Reinforce your strengths and abilities, and deflect anything that diminishes your sense of your higher purpose.

As you open up and express your Higher Self, you open yourself to accelerated lessons and growth experiences. You may find yourself facing some difficult teachers among the people with whom you come in contact. You may find yourself confronting issues you'd prefer to keep quietly buried. We often encounter emotional manipulation when we have resisted letting go and moving forward or when we have missed opportunities to face a particular lesson.

Free yourself from the attitude that internalizes every situation and interaction. Remember that the people with whom you interact have their own challenges and driving forces. You are not always at the center of their decisions. Be kind to yourself and be understanding of others. If it is time to remove yourself from a situation or relationship, do so. Ask for internal guidance. If there is no need to remain in an uncomfortable, unsupportive relationship, job, or circumstance, get out and move on to the next step.

MEDITATION

I seek and find wisdom during times of change. I seek and find within change the opportunity to be more fully myself.

23

TATE

WIND

Self-expression

I have one name, but I am many. I am the winds that come from all sides, from between the Four Directions. I scatter your energies and thoughts as I scatter the seeds of confusion and doubt. I bring you to your center only after you have spun like a top trying to catch me. Me! I am many! You reach out to grab me and your hand stays empty. I am quick—quicker than you.

TRADITION

Tate of the Sixteen Great Mysteries, who blows the Seed of Life across the earth, set apart from himself Tate the Supernatural, in whose negative wind blows the seed of discord. The positive side of Tate will be known in full measure in the form of a prophet who will teach us to heal with Sound.

THE CARD

You need to consider vocalizing your questions or feelings. Use sound as a means of expressing your emotions, either verbally, through yelling, chanting, or singing a particular sound, or perhaps by banging a drum or using another musical instrument. Let the vibrations of the sound you make shake up the tension and anxiety you've been holding inside. Allow the wind to carry the sound waves into the earth where they can be absorbed. The intention is not always to keep quiet but to "let it out" and hear the sound of that release. The release gives you the opportunity to experience the liberating supernatural breath in many ways.

If you are angry, express your feelings to the listening Spirit before confronting an individual or situation. Doing so allows you to express yourself with clarity. See that your anxiety and anger do not destroy your power to handle and resolve the situation effectively.

MEDITATION

Through times of discord and confusion, I seek the steady center within myself for stability, guidance, and grace.

24

YUMENI

WHIRLWIND & STORM

Focus

I travel this earth according to the Eight Winds, that you may see the power of each, that you may know the gifts of each. Life's travels lie not along a straight course but across expanses of rippling change, endless opportunities to learn. Each learning provides an opportunity to direct and focus the energy that surrounds you and flows through you. You may choose, as I do, to follow the path of the life-giving waters.

TRADITION

Yumeni is a Supernatural Spirit who travels the Four Winds and the Four Directions, creating tornadoes and earthquakes. Yumeni Whouha, the Material, split herself so as to be either positive or negative; Yumeni the Supernatural is that negative. Abundance can be destroyed by bad weather.

THE CARD

You may be trying to accomplish too many things, spinning in many directions at once without clear intent. Stop; focus on the primary goal or purpose. Are you trying to walk along several roads at once, without seeing how they intersect? Examine the directions in which you are unnecessarily expending energy. Choose a single path and walk in the direction it leads you. Concentrating on one path allows you to see it more fully and to appreciate the atmosphere surrounding you, giving you greater insight and assurance with each step. This commitment to your chosen path unites you with your inner guidance, keeping you on track to learn your lessons, experience your successes, and share your gifts.

MEDITATION

Through the many demands and distractions, I learn to focus, and step by step I learn my direction and achieve my goal.

PART III

THE ELEMENTS OF
THE SWEAT LODGE

25

MAHPIA

CLOUD

Compulsions/Addictions

I am cold and distant. The only heat I know is that of Wakinyan when he chooses to wrap himself within me. I am loose and unformed, at the mercy of the wind. A vehicle of others' ways, I travel continent to sea to continent, bringing nourishment or despair. I wish for you, as for myself, wholeness. You may see a cloud when you look upon me, but know that I am only a servant, without direction.

My expression is that of others. My true being is unformed.

TRADITION

Tate, Wind, sent his eldest son, Eya, to form the first Cardinal Point in the West. Disobeying his father, Eya went up to the mountain where Wakinyan, Thunder-being, lives. As punishment, he now travels across the earth as Mahpia, Cloud. Mahpia brings the shadow across the Sun and the rain, snow, hail, and sleet. Within this cloud, as thunder and lightning, travels Wakinyan, hidden from human eyes.

THE CARD

It is time to learn from your addictions, to begin to resolve dissolute habits in order to realize the true dimensions of your personal power. Compulsions and addictions cast a dark shadow over life, blocking your view of your soul's purpose, clouding your focus, and closing in your perspective.

Dispel the cloud hovering overhead and begin taking steps toward release from the major compulsions in your life. Determine the internal and external support you require. Surround yourself with positive people who will encourage you. Free your mind and spirit so you can soar.

It is your right to live unshackled and uncontrolled by any addiction. Make a commitment to improve your life, releasing the disintegrated old to create a space for the solid, the new.

MEDITATION

I find the strength to face my compulsions, to claim life over death, to claim wholeness over disintegration.

26

SAPA

THE WEST—BLACK

Meditate

I stand at the origins of the West, of darkness, of inner time. I give pause, strengthening retreat from the world of time. Avail yourself of my gift. I bring you a special peace. Seek me in the dark and know comfort, not fear. Seek me in the spaces between words. Seek me between the footfalls upon earth. I am there.

And I love you.

TRADITION

Yata, the second of Tate's five sons, took Eya's first and honored place and was sent to the West, where the sun sets and the day ends, to create the first Cardinal Point. It is the direction of the Winged Ones and the Thunderbeings. Sunset is the time for spiritual ceremonies, when we communicate with the Spirit World. The West is represented by the color black.

THE CARD

We are flooded by influences, interactions, and stimuli each day. It's important to take periodic breaks from the fast pace of our lives and return our attention to the quiet place where the Spirit rests. Let the sun set on the rest of your day and the turmoil of your life. Find the time and place to meditate. Meditation is a path toward yourself, a means of learning to listen to self-guidance. This is your time to communicate with Spirit and open to your inner self.

MEDITATION

I honor the Spirit of the West. I open myself to the gifts of darkness, of silent retreat.

27

LUTA

THE NORTH—RED

Renewal

I am the North. I am that peace that comes to all of you in time. See me now, hear me now, and share in this treasure. Should you visit with me, you would find strength of knowledge, the sure-footedness shown by those animals who live in the North. I live in a place of endings and beginnings, of change at the core. I wish for you to know your way to me, that you may be made wise, skillful, and strong on the path you follow.

TRADITION

Wazi Yapa, son of Tate, Wind, was sent to the North, the direction of The Whirlwind and home of the Vital-izers, to create the second Cardinal Point. From the North comes the changing wind as well as winter. Winter snow purifies Mother Earth and puts her to sleep so that she can rest, building the energy to bestow the beauty and blessings of spring. The North is represented by the color red.

THE CARD

You have been expending energy freely in many areas of your life. Now, before committing your exertions to future endeavors, take time for contemplation. Regain the strength you will need. Renewal means reacquaintance with the energy within you.

Nurture yourself—provide yourself with what you need physically, mentally, and spiritually. Filter out debil-itating thoughts and concentrate on putting healthy foods into your system. During this time of renewal, reevaluate the way you expend your energy. Slow down, examine your needs, and look within. Get the rest you require and spend more time alone, and you will come back strong, with restored vigor and drive.

MEDITATION

I honor the Spirit of the North. I open myself to the gifts of wisdom, vitalization, and completion.

28

GI

THE EAST—YELLOW

Clarity

I am the doorway of the Sun.

I am where Wi meets with the world in the full power of his blessings.

I open myself to you in celebration of this blessing, this miracle.

I offer you each day the new beginning.

Know, children of the Earth, that you may call on me at any time.

I welcome you.
I exist as an entity that you may experience.

TRADITION

Yap, son of Tate, Wind, was sent to the East to create the third Cardinal Point. It is the direction of the rising sun, bringing a new day, clarity, and enlightenment. The East is represented by the color yellow.

THE CARD

The light has risen; you can now begin to see your life with clarity, a new light. A new day dawns and you arise with courage, ready to make a fresh start. This is an opportunity to transform your way of looking at things, to broaden your view and expand the scope of your awareness. Now is a time of inspiration: The prospect before you is clear and unobscured. Understanding all that takes place around you, journey onward, past limitations.

MEDITATION

I honor the spirit of the East. I open myself to the gifts of new beginnings, of clarity and illumination.

29

OKAGA SKA

THE SOUTH—WHITE

Growth

I am Okaga, son of Tate, sent forth to a place that was empty. I took a stance and created there a doorway between those with form and those without. Honor those not yet born and those who have left you. They live for a time in this place, and the doorway is an open one. Do you remember sensing, when you were very young, spirits passing by you? You knew it as a right and natural thing.

Now you call yourselves wise because you have

*survived some of life's trials; but have you forgotten
the wisdom of my gift, the open eye of the untaught
child? This open eye receives great knowings of self,
the world, and the worlds beyond. It is the eye of
creation as shared by my father, Tate, through me.
Receive this gift again—now—and rejoice in it! It is
the energy that blesses your Mother Earth with the
warmth to bear abundant life.*

TRADITION

Tate, Wind, sent his youngest son, Okaga, to create the
last Cardinal Point in the South. It is the direction of the
Spirit World and the world beyond. From the South come
the warm winds that enable Mother Earth to bear her
fruits so that she may sustain life. The South is represented by the color white.

THE CARD

The internal work you've been doing has paid off.
Congratulations! You are about to experience the next
level of growth and will now be rewarded with new
ideas, new sensibilities, and new vitality. By setting aside
old patterns, you have cleared ground for the growth
that will be yours. Your determination has led you to this
point and will serve you well in the future. Let this experience reinforce your future growth and change.

MEDITATION

I honor the Spirit of the South. I open myself to the
gifts of innocence, of new growth and rejuvenation.

INIPI

SWEAT LODGE

Purification

Each day you may be made anew. The power of my gift is so strong, all is cleansed away and all emerges in newness. Your heart will beat like a newborn's and your stomach will cry out for nourishment. You will lay your head against your mother's breast and your needs will be satisfied.

Women, honor yourselves. Know that, in its female wisdom, your body cleanses you each

Moontime. Hold that time sacred, apart, and listen to your deepest voice.

Men, I bring this gift that you may enter into this holy place and release the dust and ashes of past days in the way that renews; that you may walk in balance with your sisters, maintain your ties to your Mother, and always know the love of Wakan Tanka.

TRADITION

The Inipi ceremony was brought by Kanka to the people as a way for them to restore themselves to the full life of Spirit. The ceremony connects all of creation. Fire, water, earth, and air all share in the re-creation of the Earth Mother's womb, from which we come. Crawling in on all fours, one acknowledges one's relationship to all living things. Within the Lodge exists the opportunity to redress imbalances and receive anew the gift of life.

Traditionally, this ceremony of purification precedes all other ceremonies and events of importance; it is also used in healing.

THE CARD

The Inipi ceremony was given to men and women so they could purify themselves spiritually, physically, mentally, and emotionally. One enters the womblike lodge to be purified and reborn. We learn appreciation of the elements—air, water, fire, earth. In the darkness, we are connected with all our brothers and sisters on earth. We are all one people.

Take steps to purify yourself on all levels, to prepare yourself to take your place in the whole of life. Purification helps bring you closer to others, cures your anger, fear, hatred, and all such blocks to unity. Forgiveness and understanding are basic: accepting the individuality and uniqueness of each.

Look within and recognize the aspect of your life in greatest need of purification. What emotions or thoughts act as barriers to your growth in this area? Gently replace these barriers with positive thoughts, and support yourself with an open heart. Let love and forgiveness guide your way.

MEDITATION

Through the gifts of the Creator, I bring myself anew into the world, restored and balanced, keenly aware of Spirit within me and surrounding me.

31
CHUNUPA WAKAN
THE SACRED PIPE
Prayer

How can I tell you of this gift of gifts?
It is a thing beyond words,
  a promise and a way,
  a way to know.
From the Creator it comes to you.
Know the promise first as a hope within.
Know the way first as a questioning step.
Know that both will lead you to
  the center of the world.
Then you will understand.

TRADITION

The Sacred Pipe was made by the Creator and brought to the people by the White Buffalo Calf Woman. White Buffalo Calf Woman sang, "I give you this magnificent earth, on which you will live and multiply. You will walk in balance on this earth. I give you this sacred object and with it you will come to the center of the world. You will pray for the living things, those with four feet, those with two feet, those that swim, those that fly, those that crawl, and all that the Creator has given so that you might live. This is what your Grandfather has said. Only thanks to this Sacred Pipe will the Tree of Life live again."

THE CARD

The Sacred Pipe is reminding you to pray for all life, to pray when you need support. It is here for you today, to reinforce your understanding that your prayers are heard and will be answered.

Pray to your Grandfather, the Creator. Give thanks to the Four Directions, and all you require will be granted. Pray for living things—those with four feet, those with two feet, those that swim, fly, and crawl. Prayer is intricately related to one's personal growth. Let it become part of your daily routine. Prayer brings you to a state of peace, calm, and awareness of higher powers. In the process, you become centered and balanced. Let your prayers come from the heart. Remember to give thanks for all you have received.

MEDITATION

I seek to become of clear intent in all circumstances. I seek the intention of Spirit: harmony, balance, and love.

32

CHA WAKAN

TREE OF LIFE

Acceptance

In me, all life is One: There is no demarcation of "other." The nuances of vision may vary, yet the essential sap is nowhere separated, and is, in itself, exaltation. I am the bearer of this knowledge, this understanding, this experience of grace; however you may insist on believing you are apart from that which is in you, that which surrounds you, the law which is All will bring you to me, to union and communion.

I bless you.

TRADITION

The Tree of Life is the archetype of all spiritual knowledge. The trunk forms branches and the branches form leaves. Humans are like the leaves. We reach a certain ripeness, and the time comes to go into the Spirit World. Our bodies drop to the earth, like leaves of the tree.

THE CARD

The Tree of Life reminds us to be patient and accepting as we travel our spiritual path. Open your heart to all your brothers and sisters and to all of creation, relinquishing your judgments and expectations (of yourself and others). Allow all our relations to be exactly who they are; accept all that you are. We are all connected, parts of great Tree of Life in its thick foliage. Although each leaf has its own individual form and life, all grow from the same source, the same roots; all sway together in the same breezes. The tree grows strong and tall, with each leaf adding its part to the beauty of the whole. We must accept that each of us is only one leaf; by itself, one leaf does not make a tree.

MEDITATION

I honor the abundant diversity of Spirit and rejoice in my place within the fabric of creation.

33

AHPO WI CHAPI

MORNING STAR

Hope

We greet you with joy, to shine upon your world as it shifts from darkness to light. You must feel peace in that time of change. It is a patient time, when paths open briefly to allow broadening experiences. The time is a gift that we are blessed to share in with you. Partake of much joy, much peace, much beauty, in surety, in flux. Be with us, share this time of wonder. You will learn much, and bless the whole of your day.

TRADITION

An eight-pointed star is formed by the poles at the top of the lodge, the points of which represent the eight "morning stars," the planets. They have Lakota names, but you know them better as Mercury, Saturn, Venus, Neptune, Mars, Pluto, Uranus, and Jupiter. Sometimes several of them appear in the morning, but the first one to show itself will be the Morning Star.

THE CARD

A light has appeared beneath the darkness to illuminate your way. This light shines upon you and upon those areas of your life that have darkened your journey. It is time to come out of the darkness and allow support, guidance, and love. You can see the brilliance ahead of you as you walk with confidence and trust in the future. Let this Morning Star shine into your consciousness and you will be able to meet the present and future with wonder, expecting the fulfillment of your desires.

MEDITATION

I partake of the gift of shifting light, of shadowless vision and gentle perception.

34

TUNKASILA ONIWAN

GRANDFATHER'S BREATH

Faith

I speak, as you have asked. A long time has passed since I have been asked, so I will do my best to share an understanding of myself. I am not wholly of your world. I do not often make use of words.

I am a dimension of transformation, a vehicle of transmutation, a path of release, and a channel of communication.

I am the breath of your creation. You may give your disease over to me and know relief. Through me, you may know your strength and heal from within. You may re-create yourself. This is the gift of your Creator, whose breath I am.

TRADITION

Grandfather's Breath appears in the lodge as steam. The steam dilates the pores of the skin and forces all maladies out of the body through perspiration. When the lodge door is opened, feelings and prayers escape with the steam, and the wind disperses these prayers to each of the Four Directions.

THE CARD

Grandfather's Breath is the very breath of life. Water and heat combine in Grandfather's Breath, and your prayers are invisibly carried with the steam. Faith is the ability to trust, proof unseen. It is the forerunner of brighter days and releases the soul from anxiety, stress, and turmoil. Faith that your prayers will be heard lightens your burdens, establishes a serene outlook, and allows for optimism.

Believe that you are enveloped in safety. Since we do not always have the steam of the Sweat Lodge, you may wish to burn sage or tobacco as you pray, trusting that the smoke produced will carry your prayers to Wakan Tanka.

MEDITATION

I honor the many opportunities given to me to restore my well-being.

35

PEJUTA WAKAN

SACRED HERBS

Healing

We speak to you from underfoot, from the side of the roadway, from unpeopled places. We are always here, right where you need us to be. This is our way and our blessing, for we, too, are your relatives. We grow from Mother Earth side by side with you. Whatever your need, there is one of your plant relatives who can restore you. Each of us is unique, as you are. We have different work to do in different seasons, as you do. This is our role, which we per-

*form with great respect and joy. Each of us has spe-
cial reason for living, as you do. We are not so different from you after all. We seek to ease your way.*

TRADITION

The most beautiful prayer is purification with an herb
such as sage or cedar. To purify oneself in this way is
equal to hours of prayer. Each herb carries its own healing properties and powers. Some of the herbs used in the
Sweat Lodge ceremony are sweet grass, which invokes
positive and negative spirits; cedar, which is used to bless
the rocks and in loading the Sacred Pipe; and sage, which
chases away negative spirits and, when placed in contact
with the hot stones, heals respiratory problems and colds.

THE CARD

You are being asked either to accept healing that will
come your way or to offer healing to someone in need.
Healing can take place on many levels and may be
offered in many ways. Allow whatever healing is appropriate for you. Ask for what you need, but do so without
expectation or limitation. You may ask for healing in a
particular area and, to your surprise, healing of an even
deeper wound will occur, healing more integral to your
overall growth and development.

Among the agents of greatest healing are self-accep-
tance, self-forgiveness, and self-esteem. Healing your
belief system is the first step in healing yourself physically, spiritually, emotionally, and mentally.

MEDITATION

I give thanks to my little sisters, the healing plants. I recognize our relationship and honor their great and gentle work.

36

CHANLI WAPAKTA

PRAYER TIES

Social Consciousness

*We convey the essence of the Circle of Creation.
We carry prayer to the heart of Creation. We remind
you of the Grandfather's blessed promise to the
Buffalo Nation, that they always hear your prayers.
Through us, the circular vision of oneness teaches
you to release your grip on the old matter of creation and extract new form. Pray, then, for your
sisters and brothers, the elders, the children, the
unborn, the ancestors who gave you life. Pray for*

the Mother of all, Maka, and for all that draw life from her body. Pray for the whole of what you know and for that which is beyond. And always, always, give thanks. This is the prayer of the Creator. This is the Circle of Life.

TRADITION

When we make prayer ties, we are taking the opportunity to offer our prayers for others. Prayer ties are made by stringing together little packets of cloth filled with tobacco. As each packet is made, a prayer is offered. The ties are brought into the lodge during the Inipi ceremony.

THE CARD

It is time to shift your attention from your own concerns to what you can do for humanity. Spend time praying for others. Send healing energy into the world. What gifts or traits do you have to offer? What role is appropriate for you to play, given your personal interests and individual circumstances? Find an activity that will give you the opportunity to experience joy while doing something useful. Work at becoming tolerant and understanding, of yourself and others. Allow yourself to forgive, through love and compassion. Create joy by giving without expectation. Rewards will be gained by those who serve.

MEDITATION

Through service, I come to know the Beauty of Spirit and the joy of life.

37

OLOWANPI

SACRED SONGS

Harmony

*We, the keepers of the sacred songs, greet you.
Song is a language older than any living tongue. The
sacred songs of all times and nations contain within
their music and harmonies great knowledge from the
realm of Light. The reverberation of the notes within
your body awakens memory and wisdom, clears the
channels of energy, and brings about harmony within the individual cells and all that has been created.*

Unity is established through focus of spirit, mind, and body, enabling the singers of these most powerful songs to sustain truth within the world. We, the keepers of these songs and the songs of all the spirit circles, sing with you. We join our vibrations with yours: Truly, your voice is heard among the stars.

TRADITION

The sacred songs are teachings about the essence of life. Each song contains a fundamental understanding, and even if this understanding is defined in different ways by different individuals, the teaching does not vary. The basis of Lakota spiritual teaching is love, humility, patience, and respect for others and oneself.

THE CARD

Walk with inner guidance in harmony with your environment and with others. Obstacles facing you begin to disintegrate. What you have been working toward is now within your reach. You begin to see how you fit into your surroundings and to acknowledge your role within the chord and measure.

MEDITATION

I raise my voice in praise, and joy flows through my being.

38

PITA HOCHOKAN

THE FIRE PIT

Motivation

I am the void that brings forth; I am the Circle of Creation; I am the place and the voice of the sacred fire. I am Maka, transformed for your ceremony of cleansing fire. Within my cup of being find you the very clear message of life. I am the circular vessel, the home of this truth.

TRADITION

During the Sweat Lodge ceremony, the fire pit symbolizes the Sun, who gives his energy to the Earth. Stones are here for the ceremony.

THE CARD

Just as the Sweat Lodge ceremony begins at the fire pit with the energy of a flame, your new endeavors begin with your motivation. The mettle and attentiveness generated by personal motivation carry you forward to completion, to the achievement of your goal. Your inner fire propels you forward, giving you a clear vision of the desired outcome. Carry that vision through to the end, and you will be strong and swift as wildfire.

If there is something in your life you are attempting without success, consider the strength of your motivation. See if you can ignite your interest. If you cannot get "fired up" about it, maybe it's time to let it go.

MEDITATION

I spend quiet time within the void that gives forth, propels my creativity, and inspires my actions.

39

MITAKUYE OYASIN

ALL MY RELATIONS

Respect

*Bring to your mind and actions that which is
    known in your heart.*
Bring to your lips that which sings within.
Bring to your hands that which touches within.
Bring to your feet that which moves within.
Bring to your eyes the vision from within.
Allow the inner world life in the manifest.
This is my message to you.

TRADITION

Mitakuye Oyasin is a prayer recognizing the oneness of all creation and our relationship with all two-leggeds, four-leggeds, fish, birds, insects, rock people, and the trees and plants.

THE CARD

Honor all forms of life and the oneness of all creation. Begin by respecting yourself, your needs, your emotions, thoughts, and ideas. Then, invite all your earthly brothers and sisters into the great Circle of Life. Showing respect for all forms of life means honoring our individuality as well as our unity. We are all created of the same Source and share the earth together as family. Through respect, we live in mutual harmony.

Regard the individual growth and life cycle of each being, its time to receive and its time to give, its time of sacrifice to help sustain the lives of others. When we burn sage, we give thanks for the sacrifice it has made for the good of all. When any creature eats to sustain its life, it is able to do so through the sacrifice of another's life. And when we die, we nourish the earth, providing new life and growth.

MEDITATION

I seek and find my ties of kinship with all life. I honor my relatives by living lightly on the earth.

40

HOCHOKAN WAKAN

SACRED MOUND

Reverence

*From the heart of the sacred Lodge I am formed.
Beside the doorway to the womb of the Mother you
may leave behind you in a sacred manner those
objects that are your holy tools. I am the place of
reverence. As you pass by me, I call out your name,
and, in the gathering power of the Spirits, you are
recognized and acknowledged. Thus are you prepared to enter the sacred space of the Inipi.*

TRADITION

The sacred mound is an altar placed to the right of the lodge door, where sacred objects are placed during the Inipi ceremony. It is made to represent Mole, Earth's guardian, and is formed from the earth dug out of the center of the lodge to make the hole where the heated rocks will be placed.

THE CARD

As you tend the altar of life, you are surrounded by spiritual support and protection. It is within the air you breath, the sky above, and the earth below. Personally symbolic objects come into your life as visible, tangible signs of the grace and power that are your natural birthright. Regard these sacred objects and your sanctified space with respect and reverence. Let your sacred objects become part of your ritual of prayers. Allow your reverence for these holy objects to teach you to revere all life, and have faith that it will help you balance the spiritual and physical in yourself. Remember to pray for the healing of others.

MEDITATION

I attend to my life with reverence, reverence that comes from the heart.

41

MINI

WATER

Creativity

I am clarity and purity; therefore I am cleansing.
I am liquid and flowing; therefore I am change.
I bring forth life; therefore I am creativity.
I sustain life; therefore I am nurturing.
Even before your birth, I supported and nurtured
you: I am the blood of your Mother, Maka. Taking
many forms, I challenge and sustain you. Ever in
motion, giving and taking. From me vast creations
emerge.

TRADITION

Water, one of the four elemental spirits, creates and sustains life. Our bodies are composed largely of water, so that we can remain pure. During the Inipi ceremony, water is poured on the hot rocks in the lodge, uniting the water of life and the spirit of our Grandfather, the rock. This creates the steam that purifies us, body, mind, and spirit.

THE CARD

You are comfortable in the flow of life, so you move fluidly along your path, expressing yourself freely with words, images, sounds, movement, or just in the way you create what you want in your life. Now you are being given the opportunity to create the future. Leave the past behind, and take with you only what will nourish your future creativity.

MEDITATION

I release myself into the moment, into the flow of time, events, cycles, and emotions, and I find grace and fertile ground along the way.

NIYAN

AIR

Life Force

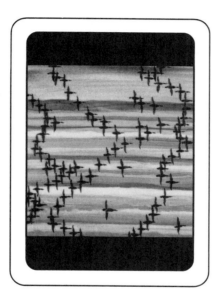

As one of the four sacred elements, I support and sustain you. The motion of Skan speaks to you through me, as I am ever changing. Yet I lead you to the One Source, for the breath you draw to sustain your own physical being is shared by the entire world. Think on this.

My path leads directly to the One who loves you. Know this, and acknowledge your Source with each breath. Inhale the life force of the dream from

which you come. Feel me as I permeate each cell of your body. Recognize the presence of all who share in this dream. Exhale this love into your world.
   This is my gift to you.

TRADITION
Air is one of the four elemental spirits. The air that we breathe is the soul of the individual, the soul of humanity. It is the essence of our spirit. The Creator is in each breath of air we take into our lungs. He is in us and everywhere, the negative and positive of Life. The air we breathe has been used and recycled by another life before us—maybe by a fly or a plant, a fish or a dinosaur. Each breath we take springs from some part of creation.

THE CARD
Breathe in with gratitude and joy all that life has to offer you. Become conscious of the life-giving properties of the air surrounding you. If you'd like to do something to help the world, use your mind for thoughts of beauty, joy, peace, and love, and you'll be exhaling all these into the air, where they can circulate among your brothers and sisters on earth.

If you habitually resist living your life fully, then practice breathing in air a little at a time, increasing the flow with each breath. Let your lungs expand with full, deep breaths; as you do, allow your consciousness of life to expand within you. Stop denying life. Enter the flow of all that life has to offer. You have the right to "breathe in" all that you can and to experience the joy of being alive.

Breath is like a prayer. The Creator is in each breath you take, and your thoughts and intentions are in each exhalation. In times of stress, breathe deeply; concentrate on your breathing process, letting the air circulate throughout, relaxing each part of your body in turn.

You share the same air with all living things, and there is enough for everyone.

MEDITATION

Within each breath, I inhale the gift of life and exhale the gift of myself into the world.

43
PITA
FIRE
Eternal Life

Gaze into my being. Few of you can resist, for I speak strongly to your core and history of your being. Of the sacred four, I support you and sustain you.

Behold my strength, my power to transform. I am here always to teach you the Road of Life. Do I sustain life and take life? No. I am life. Keeping balance, reshaping the landscape, renewing your

Mother and your soul, for know that there is no end, only change and renewal and the clarity of refining spirit into the One from which you came forth.

TRADITION

Fire represents the great power of Wakan Tanka, who gives life to all things. Like a ray of sunlight, it has the power to create and the power to consume. As one of the four elemental spirits, it can never be extinguished.

THE CARD

You are being asked to look to your inner flame, that which burns brightly for all eternity. You will leave a part of your light behind when it is your time to go to Spirit. What will you be leaving behind? What influence would you like to have on the world you will one day leave? You continually share your thoughts and words with all around you. Your thoughts are in each breath you release. Are these thoughts you want to send traveling around the world? Your words and actions are pieces of yourself that will be passed down to your children and to other people. Are these the teachings you wish to impart to the world? Examine your inner flame and determine your inner truth.

MEDITATION

My spirit lives within as the flame of Life, constantly renewing, constantly refining, providing the energy for me to walk my Earth Path.

44

MAKA

EARTH

Nurturing

I am of the four sustainers, gifts of your Mother to you that you may have life upon her body. I give you clear teaching of the way of love: Look to me, the earth, the soil. Consider of what I am made. Consider how it is that I renew myself, how it is that I bring forth new life. I live in a continual cycle of giving and receiving. My way of being, always, is the circle of love.

TRADITION

Earth is one of the four elemental spirits. The center of the lodge represents the womb of Mother Earth, who gives life to all living things. We enter the lodge to be reborn. We give thanks to Mother Earth for giving us the food on which we live.

THE CARD

Think about how to accept nurturing—from others and even from yourself. Nourishment and caring begin within. Attend to your body's needs along with your emotional and spiritual hungers. Allow yourself to accept all that you require. Listen to the needs of others and provide nurturing to them. Nurturing is a two-way process that helps us develop, grow, and sustain life. Use positive, encouraging language when describing how you are and the activities in your life. Appreciate yourself. You deserve it.

MEDITATION

The cycles of time bring me into awareness of the interdependence of all life.

45

WAGLE SHUN

THE SWAN

Peace

See my physical form.

I am grace, silent movement upon the waters of emotion.

Grace, as I and my mate entwine necks in an embrace.

I am the peace of the heart, and I present myself to you that my image may cast into your mind's eye the dream and the realization of peace.

TRADITION

The White Buffalo Calf Woman, who brought us the Sacred Pipe, has been known to present herself in the form of a swan. Her symbol is also used in many other tribes' teachings.

THE CARD

You are reminded to be at peace with all things. Find the place of peace within yourself by accepting all that you are and forgiving yourself and others. Let love take the place of fear, and allow your inner peace to gently come forth. Share this strongest beauty with the world around you. Ask yourself what you can do in your life to bring about peace. As peace grows greater, it begins to take flight, touching and uplifting all with whom you come in contact.

MEDITATION

I seek and find the state of being where the grace and beauty of all life is known. In this way is my heart filled and at peace.

46

UNCI

GRANDMOTHER

Female Power

I am the path between the fire and the door, of the sacred pattern and purpose of the Inipi, holding firm the channel by which the transforming fire enters the sacred womb of the Mother. On my back travels the energy of transformation and re-creation; on me travel the eons of the covenant between the Creator and his children. I am the bridge. I am the flow. I am the continuation of the promise. I am your Grandmother. Don't cross me.

TRADITION

The pathway called Unci runs between the fire and the
door of the lodge. Along it are carried the stones that
have been filled with the cleansing warmth of Wakan
Tanka. The path must not be crossed: To do so would be
to break the circle of the elements and to disperse the
holy power of the Inipi.

THE CARD

Whether you are a man or a woman, you are being
asked to express the feminine side of yourself. Let your
right-brain functions—intuition, feelings, and creativity—
influence your life more. Trust your instincts and listen to
your innate wisdom. Act on your "gut feelings." Faith in
the outcome of such action increases your power; the
road becomes clearer, the roadblocks disappear. You
crave outlet for your creative impulses. Consider doing a
moon meditation: At the next full or new moon, express
your intention to create during the coming month whatever it is you with to establish in your life. Then, ask for
guidance and support in achieving this vision.

MEDITATION

I claim now, through timeless reaches of creation, the
strength of the feminine that is my inheritance.

47

EYESHINU TI

MOONTIME

Spiritual Power

Behold the opening, the high tide of that power manifest in woman. Now, the unformed matter of life flows from Creation's ready womb.

This is your moontime, issuing purified life energy into the world. Blessed be woman, gifted with such enduring experience! May she hold herself in honor always, protected and apart at the time of her flowing, when her power is so great it can shatter existing forms. This is a gift to the female, that her body is a vessel of spiritual power.

Moontime is a time to retreat, to meditate and understand this power—that the same power creates all form. Even when it is not forming a new human being, the power is there at woman's direction, to give birth to that which she desires.

Use this power with the wisdom offered you by the opening. Meditate and pray and bring forth beauty.

TRADITION

Moontime is a sacred time of purification. Lakota tradition considers the spiritual power of a woman during her moontime to be extremely strong. During her monthly period, a woman does not participate in communal ceremonies. Rather, she stays separate in an honored position in the moon lodge.

THE CARD

This is a sacred time for you. Turn your attention to resources of soul that are yours. Your spiritual abilities are far greater than you have imagined. It is time to accept more fully the divine you within, your connection to all things seen and unseen.

Allow your spiritual force to flow into creative and loving acts. Trust in your ability to reach new spiritual insight as you remain mindful of your joy and your highest purpose.

Use this time to draw power from our Mother. Stay

aware of the earth; keep yourself grounded as you reach for your personal heights. Go outside and soak up bountiful earth energy. Take a walk in a field, absorb the rhythm of a stream, or walk among the trees as brother or sister to them.

MEDITATION

I retreat to hear the voices of Grandmother Moon, of Mother Earth: I emerge strong with the knowledge of my history and my power.

48

WAHINHAYA

THE MOLE

Regeneration

I am the guardian of the Earth. I live beneath the surface of the earth in close communion with the Mother. All movements of the earth I know—the earthquakes and volcanoes, the storms and the gentle rains, the scattering of seeds. I know the roots within the soil and the plants upon which your foot falls. I cannot see and therefore cannot prejudge, but I glean all through the intimacy of touch and smell and taste. I know the secrets of healing, both

physical and mental, and these gifts I offer you who are your Mother's children. At the time of your Spirit's flight, I will allow your body to re-enter her great one, to nourish her who gave you life.

TRADITION

Mole guards the Earth and knows all the Earth's movements. The power of Mole is to cure through the knowledge of healing roots and plants. By picking up subtle information from nature, Mole knows what to expect in the future.

THE CARD

This is the point at which to examine your life, detach your interests from the ways of the past, and re-create your Self. You are the guardian of your Self. Come up above ground into the light. Live in the present by incorporating your knowledge and vision of past and future. Each new moment is an opportunity to awaken to Self and burrow deeper into Earth's goodness. You have the power to heal your life and create yourself anew in any moment. Listen to the messages you receive from above guiding you toward the whole healing of your body, mind, and soul.

MEDITATION

I learn of my intimate connection with Mother Earth and all her children and know my life to be one within the symphony of creation. I learn the ebb and flow, the integration and balance of all life.

49

HANBLECHEYA

CRYING FOR A DREAM

Vision

We pull you away from the world with quiet, incessant whispers, urging you forward, deeper, higher, fuller. You become aware of the need to retreat from the noise of the world, the influence of others' truths surrounding you. Finally, the pull must be allowed, and releasing for a time the comforts and securities of your known world, you lay yourself open to the elements, to yourself, to Spirit,

*to dark and to light, to the whole of time, to the
uniqueness of your existence.*

*We bid you, come with your fears and your
courage to receive the gifts of Vision, to return with
clear eyes to your walk along Earth's path.*

TRADITION

To the Lakota, visions are prophetic links to the future:
dialogues with the Creator. Visions are sought and
encountered in many ways, and, for great and serious
intentions, an individual may embark on a Vision Quest.
A boy goes on a Vision Quest at puberty to find his identity, name, and direction. The seeker undertaking the quest
isolates himself for four days and four nights on top of a
hill without food and water. The site is selected and protected by a Medicine Man. When the seeker descends
from the mountain, he goes first to the Sweat Lodge to
tell of his experience and vision, and the Wichasha Wakan
interprets and helps him understand it. Prayers, feasting,
and the distribution of gifts are the proper ending to this
ceremony.

THE CARD

Take notice of your inner promptings: A vision is gathering. A time of retreat may now be required to allow the
voices within and without to be heard.

Prepare for this communion by following your instincts.
Perhaps what is required is as simple as a half-hour soak
in the tub to release stress and confusion. Perhaps a week-
end retreat from the artificial into nature will ground your

senses and expand your consciousness. Before, during, and after a traditional Vision Quest, take care to find human guidance and make proper preparations.

Retreat to the unexplored solitude of your inner knowing, discover the appropriate path to take to heal, to strengthen, and to become clear-eyed. Bring these gifts back to the world: The whole world receives your gift.

MEDITATION

I honor the voice of the Creator within me by allowing the space for it to be heard and having the courage to act on its guidance.

PRONUNCIATION GUIDE

A brief approximation to Lakota pronunciation is as follows:

a is broad as in *father*

e is pronounced *ay* as in *pray*

i is pronounced *ee*

u is pronounced *oo* as in *cook*

c is pronounced *ch*

g between vowels is pronounced *kh* (like German *machen*)

j is pronounced *zh* as in *fusion*

n following a vowel is not pronounced as the *n* sound in English, but nasalizes the vowel, as in French: e.g., *an* is pronounced as in French *blanc*.

Source: *The Lakota-English Dictionary*, edited by Rev. Eugene Buechel S. J. (Pine Ridge, S. Dak.: Red Cloud Indian School, 1970).

SUGGESTED READINGS

Brown, Joseph Epes, ed. *The Sacred Pipe: Black Elk's Account of the Seven Rites of the Oglala Sioux*. Norman, Okla.: University of Oklahoma Press, 1953.

Erdoes, Richard, and Alfonso Ortez. *American Indian Myths and Legends*. New York: Pantheon, 1984.

Lame Deer, Archie Fire, and Richard Erdoes. *A Gift of Power*. Santa Fe, N. Mex.: Bear & Company Publishing, 1992.

Lame Deer, John Fire, and Richard Erdoes. *Lame Deer, Seeker of Visions*. New York: Simon & Schuster, 1972.

Walker, James R. *Lakota Myth*. Lincoln, Nebr.: University of Nebraska Press, 1983.

INDEX